MW01037968

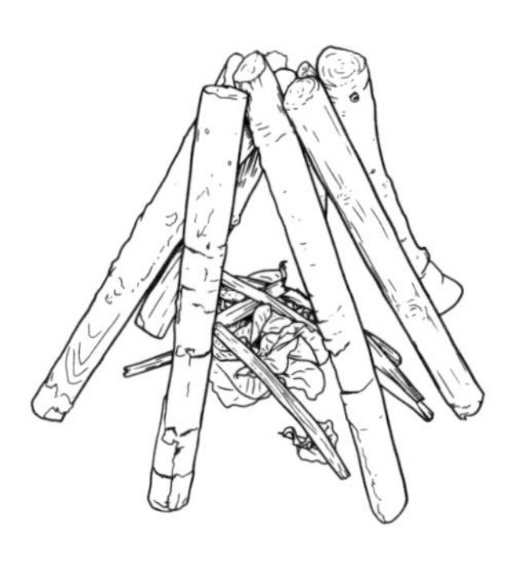

THE BOOK OF BUILDING FIRES

HOW TO MASTER THE ART OF THE PERFECT FIRE

S. COULTHARD

ILLUSTRATIONS BY
CLAIRE MCCRACKEN

CHRONICLE BOOKS
SAN FRANCISCO

First published in the United States of America in 2018 by Chronicle Books LLC.

Text first published in the United Kingdom in 2017 by Head of Zeus.

Library of Congress Cataloging-in-Publication Data
Names: Coulthard, Sally, author.
Title: The book of building fires / S. Coulthard.
Description: San Francisco : Chronicle Books, 2018. |
Includes index.
Identifiers: LCCN 2017045314 | ISBN 9781452170756
(hardcover : alk. paper)
Subjects: LCSH: Firemaking. | Stoves, Wood. | Campfires.
Classification: LCC GN417 .C68 2018 | DDC 796.54/5--dc23
LC record available at https://lccn.loc.gov/2017045314

Manufactured in China.

Design by Alice Chau.
Illustrations by Claire McCracken.

10 9 8 7 6 5 4 3

Chronicle Books LLC
680 Second Street
San Francisco, CA 94107
www.chroniclebooks.com

For my brother, Ben

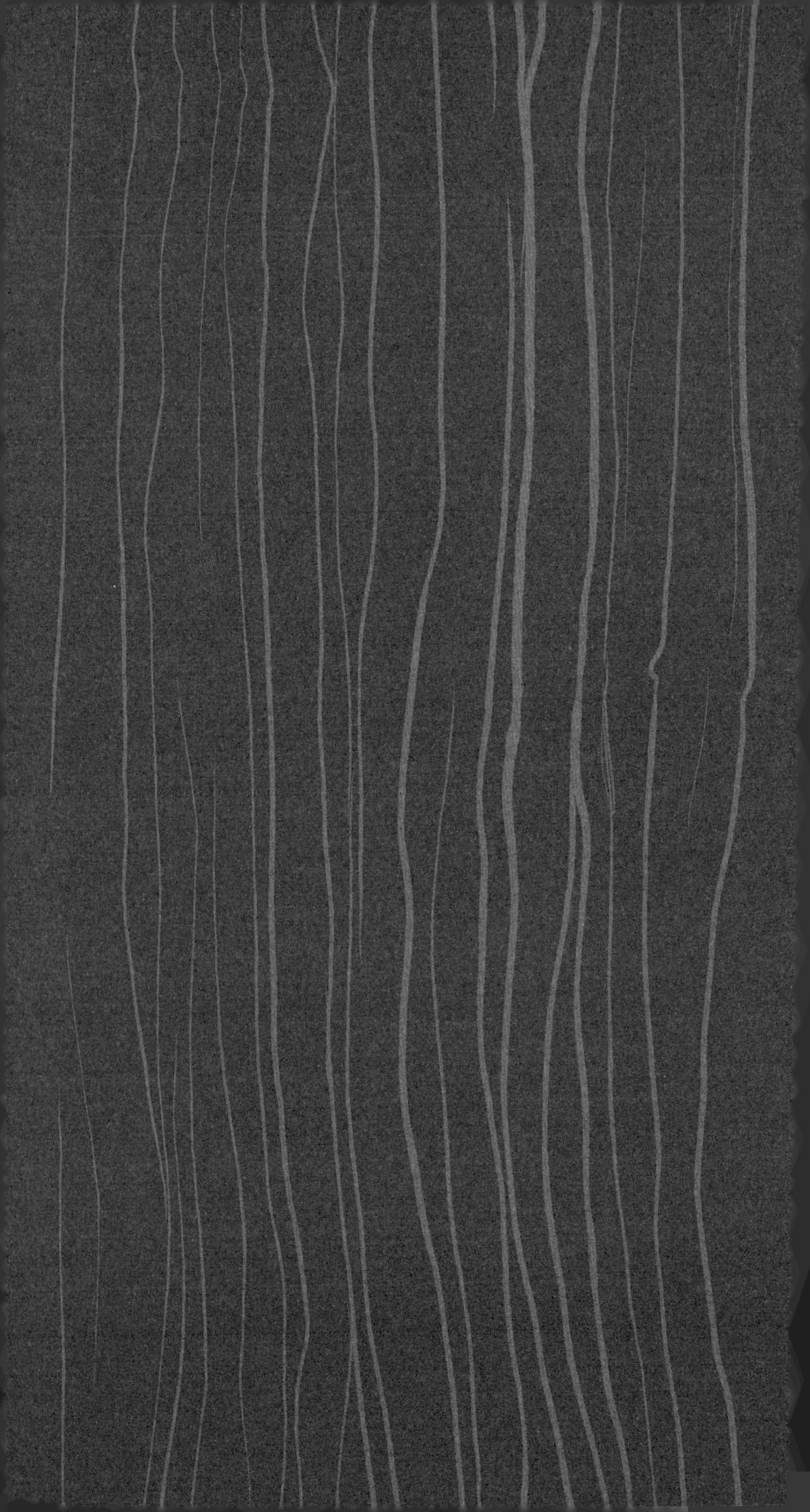

INTRODUCTION

The Ritual of Fire

"Give me," said Joe, "a good book, or a good newspaper, and sit me down afore a good fire and I ask no better."

—CHARLES DICKENS, *GREAT EXPECTATIONS*

My oldest memories are touched by fire. The sweet smell of woodsmoke takes me straight back to my childhood home, a tall Victorian townhouse blessed with fireplaces on every floor.

I'd help my father build and light the fire in the front room, a treat, because it was a space reserved for special occasions, and a great excuse to have him to myself. I learned by osmosis, slowly watching and absorbing the careful ritual of scrunching newspaper and arranging bone-dry twigs on a bed of ash. I especially liked it when he would hold a large sheet of newspaper over the mouth of the chimney to draw air up the flue. This skillful trick would transform a few infant flames into a roaring inferno in seconds—a feat both thrilling and deliciously dangerous.

Fire also takes me back to playing outdoors as a child. My brother and I would sneak to the bottom of the garden, having smuggled out a box of matches, and spend dry afternoons building small campfires and setting fire to anything that came to hand. Our favorite game involved lighting long lengths of dried nettles, the stems of which would smolder like a cigarette; we'd sit around the campfire, holding them aloft like socialites, taking the occasional puff, quickly followed by a cough and splutter.

I equate fire with childhood holidays, too. Family expeditions weren't always stress free, but the best moments were the ones when we found ourselves around a campfire, or cooking outdoors. From rough campsites to backyard sleepovers with friends, evenings were always sweeter with an open fire and convivial conversation. We'd spend summers with an Italian family, making campfires in Alpine forests and cooking polenta in a huge copper pan over the embers, the careful preparation that went into making and tending the fire adding to the sense of occasion.

As an adult, my relationship with fire has mutated into something different, but no less intense. Fire has come to mean other things—romantic evenings huddled under a blanket, or the irresistible draw of a welcoming pub after a wet Sunday walk. As a young adult working in London, I would escape for a few days to a remote hideout, complete with open fire—my idea of heaven. Away from the city, I could pretend I was living a different life, the ritual of setting and lighting a fire making me feel calmer and more connected with nature. I'm never surprised when people put "fireplace" on their vacation rental wish lists—a rural retreat without one seems strangely pointless.

Nowadays, I live on a farm with my young family. Fire, again, is everywhere. Bonfires are a regular event, a useful tool for clearing away the cuttings and branches that inevitably pile up. The kids have campfires in their little stretch of woodland—many a saucepan has been ruined by their attempts at hot chocolate, or failing that, they crack open a packet of marshmallows and perfect their toasting technique, which is something akin to a rotisserie.

Indoors, the farmhouse is warmed by a wood-fired biomass boiler—a temperamental affair but one that, when it works, puffs out gentle wafts of scented smoke. When the cold weather really sets in, no evening is complete without lighting up one of the woodstoves or a fireplace. Woodstoves are a completely different beast from traditional hearth fires, and it has taken a while to master the differences. What you miss in the friendly pops and crackles of an open flame you more than make up for in heat output and efficiency. I've discovered there's a place for both, and each has its charm.

There is, of course, a dark side to fire. As the old saying goes, "Fire makes a good servant but a bad master," and the potential for things to go wrong is never far away. As a parent, I wince at the thought of my children "playing" with fire the way my brother and I did, but those early lessons taught me more about the anatomy and behavior of fire than any schoolroom could have.

And that's what this book is really about. Fireplaces and woodstoves have made quite a comeback in the past few years; there are lots of reasons why, both economic and environmental, but perhaps it's also true that central heating is, well, just a bit *soulless*, and not everything worth having can come at the push of a button.

In the same way that thousands of people are rediscovering the pleasure of local produce or the satisfaction of making things with their own two hands, so too are many of us rekindling the primeval pleasure of wood fires. The very act of collecting branches and chopping logs, scrunching up newspaper, building stacks, and watching them burn triggers deeply buried memories. It all feels just so *familiar*.

But for all this enthusiasm, how many of us know how to build a fire? Would we know which kinds of trees burn best or how long logs need to be stored? Could we make our own firelighters, or build the perfect fire stack? Most of us love to toast our toes by an open fire but don't know or have forgotten how to build one and keep it alight.

That's where *The Book of Building Fires* comes in. It's time to get back to some firecraft basics. By the end of this book, I hope you'll have a better grasp of sourcing, seasoning, and storing firewood; choosing kindling and tinder; and building and lighting the perfect fire. There's also plenty about keeping safe—a lesson I've sometimes had to learn the hard way.

Nothing beats the companionable crackle of an open fire. In this world of fast-paced technology and virtual experiences, if we can stop and steal time for just one bit of slow living, let it be the enjoyment of a traditional wood fire. Build it, and you'll find yourself drawn to the flames. You'll also feel compelled to sit, stay, and talk for a while or warm your toes in comfortable silence. Above all, you'll be partaking in a ritual that's as old as humanity itself.

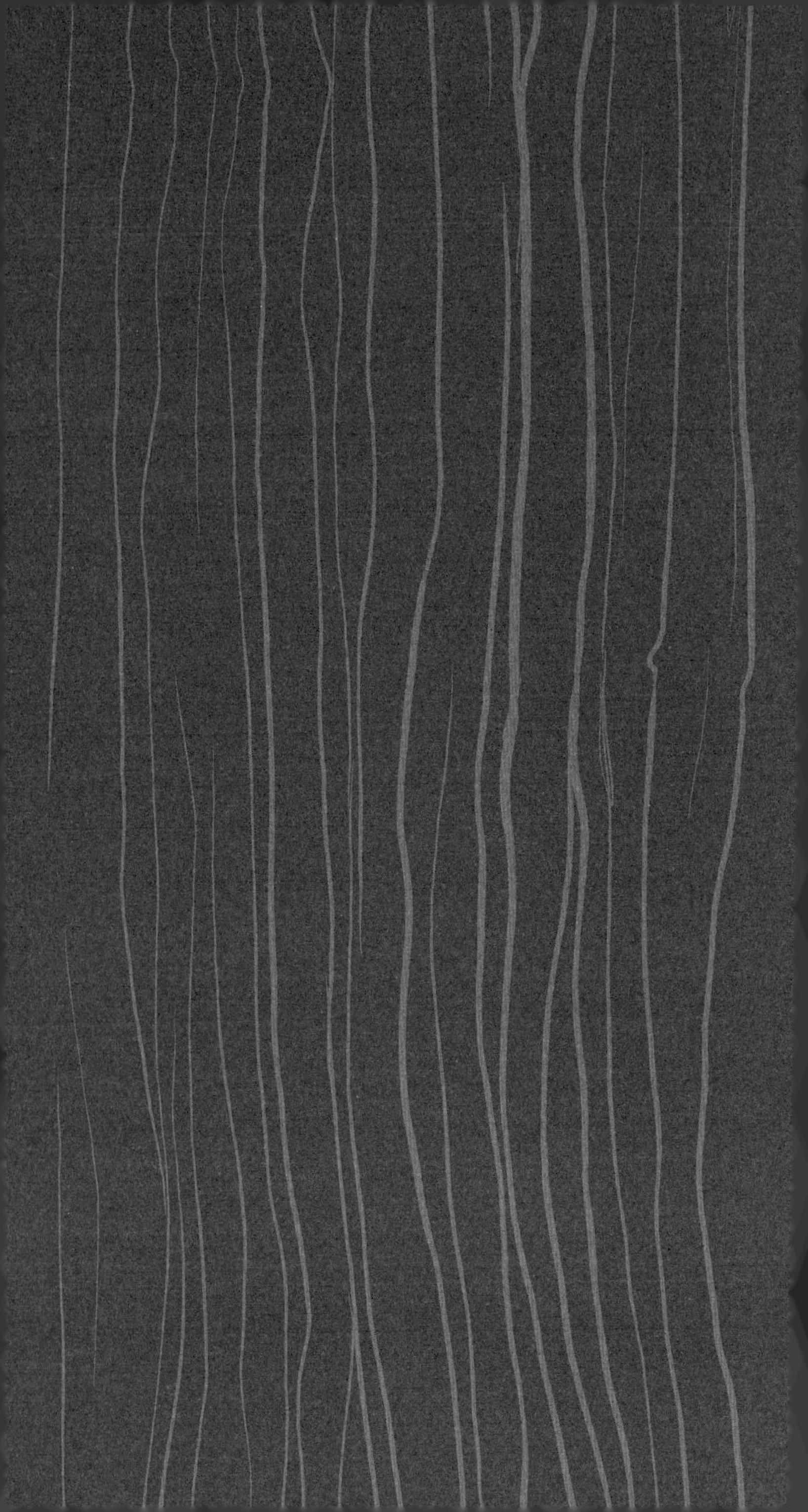

CHAPTER ONE

The Joy of Fire

Love is a smoke raised with the fume of sighs; Being purged, a fire sparkling in lovers' eyes. . .

—WILLIAM SHAKESPEARE, *ROMEO AND JULIET*

THE STORY OF FIRE

The story of fire is at the very heart of who we are. Humans are the only animals to have learned how to make fire at will. Our relationship with flames has been a long one; archaeology puts the earliest evidence of campfires a million years back, but we've been playing with fire for much longer than that. Recent studies have revealed that our primitive ape-like ancestors were probably opportunistic, scavenging "firechasers," hanging around the edges of forest fires to grab fleeing prey or pick among their cooked remains. They would have also seen the new plant growth springing up after the smoke cleared and understood the power of fire to both destroy and create life.

Learning to control fire gave humans the means to transform their diet, master the environment, and conquer new territories. Fire is warmth, protection, and safety. It has allowed us to make tools and pottery, smelt metal, and generate power. We cook, we cleanse, we purify with fire. Fire is both a warning and a welcome; it can scare away animals or invite social interaction. Fire is light, heat, smoke, and steam, the very building blocks of the industrial revolution.

But fire is also intimate. It's the tool we use to keep our loved ones warm. It represents home, hearth, and belonging. We use it to celebrate, cohere, and commemorate. We build fires for fun, for pleasure, for a break from our over-engineered lives. For all our access to technology, it seems nothing can sever our ancient ties with fire.

Throughout civilization, people have been fascinated and frightened by fire in equal measure—we use it, but we innately understand that we never truly control it. It's both lifesaver and destroyer in one. And, as humans are wont to do, what we both fear and revere we transform into something mystical. Throughout the world and history, fire has taken on deep symbolic meaning. From the phoenix in Greek mythology, which rises from the ashes to symbolize renewal and rebirth, to Vesta, the Roman fire goddess of hearth and home, many cultures have worshipped flames as a force for good. Even today, we talk of smoldering desire and hearts on fire. Love is an eternal flame; we long for someone to "light our fire." Fire is passion, courage, and energy.

But fire also scares us. We talk of fiery hells and raging infernos. People who metaphorically "play with fire" almost always get burned. Fire is fury, anger, burning hatred. We advise people against "fanning the fire" or "going down in flames." Fire is death, apocalypse, destruction. Perhaps that's why fire still has such a hold over us. We have mastered so much of our world that perhaps it does us good to have something we can't quite dominate. Fire brings us so much pleasure and comfort, but it can also thwart us and test our abilities.

FIRE NOW

Simple pleasures are making a comeback: sleeping under the stars, baking bread, crafting just for the sheer creative delight of it. Fires are a natural extension of this rediscovery. There's so much that's better about modern-day living—health, life expectancy, social mobility—and yet our genetic memory sometimes beckons us back; we feel a longing for the satisfaction that comes from performing basic, life-sustaining tasks. Gathering, chopping, and lighting your own fire gives you a sense of achievement that's difficult to rival. In a world saturated with technology and breakneck change, there's no doubt that crafting a fire makes you feel *accomplished* in a tangible, practical way.

Sitting next to a log fire, watching the flames flicker, is as close to meditation as many of us get. When we experience a roaring fire, all our senses are absorbed—this calming focus of attention takes us away from our quotidian worries, soothes our anxieties, and draws us in. It's an unconscious response, an embedded memory that reminds us that at one time fire meant heat, protection, and, above all, community. In other words, we have *evolved* to enjoy being around fires—for thousands of years, the act of building and burning a fire was the most important means of encouraging social cohesion. We may not need fire in the same critical way as our ancestors did, but few would deny that the quiet, reassuring pleasure that comes from flames is as welcome as ever.

FIRE AND NATURE

One of the wonderful bonuses of learning to build a fire is the connection it gives you to nature. Figuring out which twigs burn best, gauging wind direction, understanding the effect of weather on flames—there's a strong case to be made for picking up or dusting off some basic outdoor knowledge.

You don't have to appreciate nature to enjoy an open fire. But gaining expertise on the types of wood that burn best and how to find kindling in the forest adds immensely to the enjoyment of open fires. The act of gathering firewood brings you into contact with aspects of nature you might not have noticed or even thought about. The forest becomes a pantry of ingredients—you'll never look at cedar bark, pinecones, or dry grass in the same way again. Handle enough wood and you'll soon learn to appreciate the satisfying snap of a well-seasoned twig, or what it means when bark peels easily away in your hand.

Building fires is fun. But it's also profound. Most of us live a life divorced from our natural surroundings. By understanding and engaging with the natural world—whether it's hunting for sticks on a walk through the woods or raking the ashes into the vegetable garden—we develop a greater respect for the environment and a real sense of self-sufficiency. Get children involved and you open up a whole new world where they can build, create, and feel confidently free in their wild surroundings.

FIRE AND COOKING

On a camping trip, the evening meal, cooked over an open fire, is the highlight of the day. Campfire cooking requires total concentration—the fire is a living, changing creature, and you have to respond quickly to its moods or the food will burn. Building and managing a cooking fire takes knowledge and proficiency. Transforming raw ingredients into a hearty meal requires patience and intuition. Food that's quickly prepared and convenient often isn't appreciated; food that has taken time and skill to create is always more satisfying. But there's also an elegant simplicity to it—some of the best meals you can cook on a fire are those with just a handful of ingredients. There are few things more delicious than a pan-fried rib-eye served with fresh herbs, or buttered corn on the cob cooked in the dying embers. The fire, smoke, and setting imbue the food with an inimitable flavor and a sense of occasion that you just don't get from conventional cooking.

As children, many of us enjoyed the feeling of independence and maturity that came with campfire cooking. We might not have been allowed in the kitchen, but we could certainly rustle up a feast of marshmallows, chocolate, and graham crackers without any pesky adults getting involved. From family camping trips, to backyard adventures, to

Girl and Boy Scout outings, many of our happiest memories involve cooking over fire. If, as an adult, you can recapture even just a fragment of those first experiences, that's something worth cherishing.

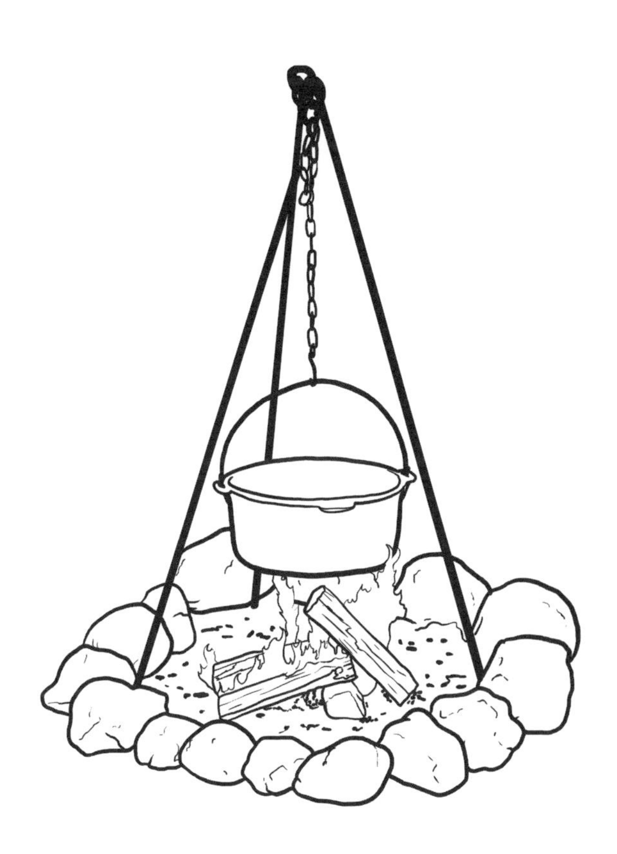

FIRE AND SURVIVAL

If you live in a rural area, power outages are all too common, especially during bad weather. It's not unusual to be left without electricity for hours, so having at least one fireplace or woodstove in your home means you'll never be cold, and you'll have the ability to bake a potato or heat water until the power returns.

Knowing how to build a fire also comes in very handy if you like camping, hiking, or any kind of adventuring on the road less traveled. If you're an active, outdoors person, the art of fire building is an essential skill; a fire can be used to signal for assistance, cook food, and keep you warm until help arrives. There's also a psychological benefit—the can-do frame of mind that comes from knowing some basic survival skills has been shown time and time again to improve the likelihood of a good outcome if you ever find yourself in a sticky situation.

This isn't a survival manual, and there are lots of books on the subject of surviving in the outdoors. What this book *will* give you is a better understanding of how fire burns, what it needs to thrive, how to create sparks, and what makes good fuel—all snippets that could just come in handy in a crisis. A little knowledge isn't always a dangerous thing.

FIRE AND THE ENVIRONMENT

The debate about whether wood fires are eco-friendly smolders on, and it can be tricky to know whether you are doing the right thing in using wood for heat. To understand the debate, you have to look at the full life cycle of a tree. It's a complex process, but in essence, as a tree grows, it absorbs carbon dioxide (CO_2) from the air. When that same tree burns or rots, it releases the same amount of CO_2 back into the atmosphere. So, whether you leave a tree to decompose on the forest floor or set fire to it, the same amount of carbon is released back into the air. In other words, wood is carbon-neutral. If we chop down and burn trees, we can also plant more—as opposed to burning coal and gas, which are both finite.

The problem comes with processing and transporting timber to your doorstep. Industrial logging, semi trucks, and gas-fueled chainsaws all contribute to timber's carbon footprint. Added to that, when wood burns at a low temperature, it releases smoke that contains small amounts of harmful pollutants, called particulates. Wood fires aren't always as ecologically friendly as we would hope.

So, what's to be done? The good news is that if you follow a BUY RIGHT, BURN RIGHT philosophy, there are few fuels that can match timber for ecological credentials, especially when we combine our ancient knowledge of seasoning wood with new, efficient woodstoves. The principles of BUY RIGHT, BURN RIGHT are:

» Gather your own wood or buy from a local supplier.
» Dry wood burns hotter and cleaner than wet wood—only use seasoned timber.
» Use woodstoves for everyday heat and fireplaces for special occasions (a fireplace burns four logs for every one in a woodstove).
» Don't burn trash, treated timber, or plastics in your fire.
» Buy the smallest woodstove you need—17,060 BTUs (5 kilowatts) is plenty for the average-size living room.
» Look for ways to improve your home's thermal efficiency. Better insulation equals less fuel needed.

FIRE AND COST

When it comes to the financials of how to heat your home, the general breakdown is as follows (although prices do fluctuate): of the three standard ways to heat a home, gas is cheapest, oil is next, and liquefied petroleum gas (LPG) and electric heating are the most expensive. On a like-for-like basis, biomass (e.g., wood pellets, chips, and logs) falls somewhere in the middle.

Few people heat their homes exclusively with wood—unless they have a biomass boiler—so for most people, the issue is whether wood is a good value as a secondary source of heating. As a rough guide, if you plan to use an average 5-kilowatt woodstove for moderate use (e.g., weekends and evenings), you'll probably need about 105 to 140 square feet (3 to 4 cubic meters) of seasoned logs over the burning season (October through March). For intensive use—morning, day, and evening—you can double that to 211 to 282 square feet (6 to 8 cubic meters). The general consensus is that running one woodstove will knock about 10 percent off the average household fuel bill, and in many cases more, especially if you have the space to store and dry cheaper, unseasoned logs.

The economics don't stack up quite as well when logs are expensive to source (such as in large urban areas); you don't have room to store wood and so can't save money by buying in bulk; or you want to heat a home with a fireplace, which burns less efficiently than a woodstove. For many people, however, the choice to enjoy a crackling fire isn't about cost. It's about the things money can't buy.

FIRE AND FUN

If your house is well served by central heating then it begs the question: why have a wood fire at all? The pleasure of a real fire is difficult to unpack—part of the satisfaction lies in creating something from nothing; other times, it's the welcome distraction that comes from focusing on a practical task. But sometimes, the reason to build a fire is just because it's fun. Not in the vacuous, commercial sense of the word, but fun in its truest form. It's genuinely life-affirming to gather in a field with friends and welcome in the stars around a roaring campfire; it's delicious to cook a freshly caught fish on shore or share a winter's evening toasting marshmallows with your smallest family members, who are still young enough to be impressed by your ability to make flames spring to life.

Part of the thrill of being on vacation, whether it's camping in the countryside or renting a cozy cabin, is that it gives us the chance to exercise our primitive fire-making muscles. We know we don't *need* fire in the same way that our ancestors did, but we certainly seem to relish the opportunity to practice it. Fire is also part of our celebratory consciousness. From bonfires to fireworks, barbecues to birthday candles, a party just isn't a party without a few sparks.

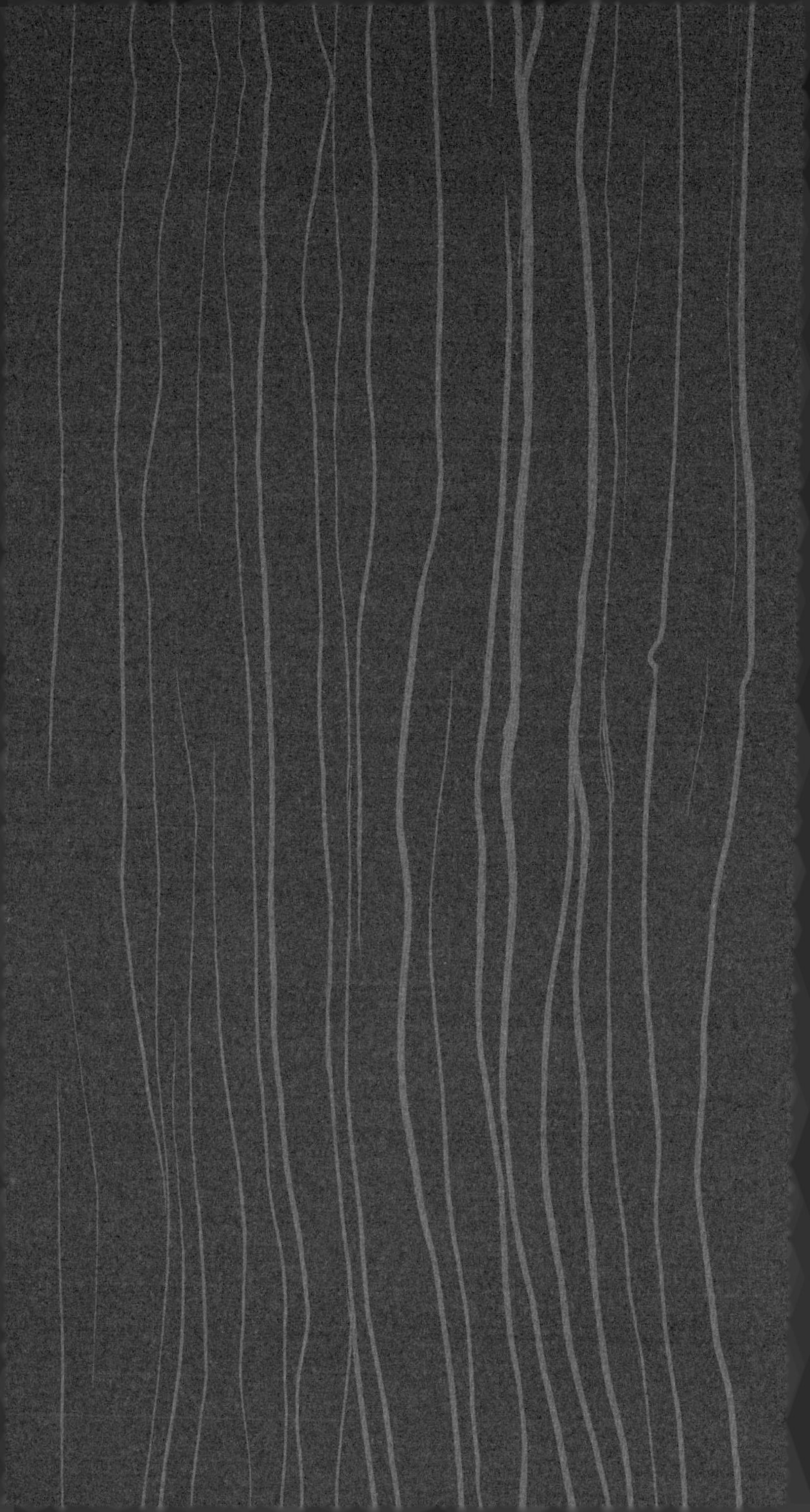

CHAPTER TWO

The Anatomy of Fire

The mind is not a vessel to be filled, but a fire to be kindled.

—PLUTARCH

HOW FIRE WORKS

Fire is a chemical reaction, one that needs three things to work—fuel, oxygen, and a source of heat. Remove any one of these three things and the fire goes out. In the case of a wood fire, the fuel is the kindling and logs, the oxygen comes from the surrounding air, and the heat comes initially from the flame of a match.

To understand how wood burns, it's helpful to think of a wood fire burning in three stages:

THE FIRST STAGE: When the fire is first lit, the logs release volatile gases and burn off any water vapor. You won't get much heat at this stage, just smoke and steam. You want to get through this stage as quickly as possible, which is why you need dry wood.

THE SECOND STAGE: When the fire really takes hold, the volatile gases start to ignite into flames and produce heat. The flames, in turn, ignite more of the logs and release more volatile gases, and the fire becomes self-perpetuating.

THE THIRD STAGE: Once the fire is really hot, and the wood has burned off all its volatile gases, you are left with char and ash. Char is almost entirely carbon and glows red hot, giving off plenty of heat without any smoke or flames. Once the fire has died out, all that's left is the ash (all the unburnable minerals from the wood, such as calcium carbonate, phosphate, and potash), which just happens to be incredible for your garden (see Ashes, page 118).

HEAT

Every fire has its own way of heating a space. Woodstoves, fireplaces, and campfires warm you in different ways:

With a woodstove, heat is transferred into your space mostly by conduction (the metal body of the stove gets very hot) and radiation (the fire emits electromagnetic waves of heat and light). What woodstoves are traditionally not so good at is convection, making hot air rise and circulate around the room. To improve convection, consider purchasing a stove fan. These nifty devices push warm air around the room using power generated from the heat of the stove. Be careful not to place too many obstacles—such as armchairs or ottomans—between you and the fireplace, as the furniture will block the radiating heat.

Fireplaces mostly rely on radiation and convection to heat the room but, because they are not encased in a metal stove, don't get much chance to conduct heat. Consider introducing a metal insert, surround, or fireback to the hearth, all of which will conduct heat or reflect it back into the room. As with the woodstove, be careful not to block the radiating heat with large furniture.

The heat from outdoor fires comes solely from radiation, as there's no metal to conduct any heat, and all the warm convected air billows straight upward into the night sky. That explains why your cheeks are always hot while your back gets cold. One way to increase an outdoor fire's heating capacity is to build a reflector next to the fire (see Which Fire to Build?, page 103).

FIRELIGHT

We know that fire is a chemical reaction that produces heat. What we often overlook, however, is fire's other useful by-product—light.

When you are planning a lighting scheme for a room, give some thought to firelight. General (or ambient) lighting provides the overall illumination for the room, and task lighting, such as a reading light, is useful for focusing on specific activities. But there's another type of lighting—decorative or accent lighting—whose sole purpose is to draw attention to a specific area or an object, or to be a feature in itself. Flames are nature's fairy lights—decorative lighting at its most captivating.

Firelight is a magical experience, a kinetic, dancing light that captures your gaze and provides endless opportunity for focus and reflection, especially in the dark. Firelight flickers and bounces off reflective surfaces; it also casts a gentle orange glow over everything it touches. With this in mind, if you are going to enjoy a fireplace, resist the urge to over-illuminate the rest of the room or you'll kill the effect. An overly bright room will strip the fire of all its cozy potential and take away its power as a focal point. Forget spotlights and overhead pendants; embrace low, subtle lighting—such as table lamps and picture lights—and make your fire the star of the show.

COMBUSTION

Once lit, a fire goes through the flaming combustion stage, when all the wood's volatile gases are burned as flames. Once this stage is completed, the fire moves on to the glowing combustion stage, when it burns as hot, glowing embers. Each stage is useful for different things—the flaming stage produces lots of light and quick heat, while the glowing stage is hotter, flameless, and more stable to cook on.

The kind of wood you use can help your fire move through the various stages more quickly or prolong them, depending on your needs. As a general rule, softwoods like pine, larch, redwood, and cedar are less dense than hardwoods and tend to burn quickly. That makes them easier to light, good for kindling, and the ideal wood for producing lots of flames. Softwoods are also cheaper and season more quickly (see Burning Hardwood vs. Softwood, page 51) but they do have a tendency to leave resin tar residues on the inside of your chimney, so be warned.

Hardwoods, on the other hand, tend to be dense and are better for emitting sustained heat over a longer period of time. They also burn down to a hot bed of embers, ideal for cooking over. Hardwoods are more expensive (because they take longer to grow) but burn more cleanly. Regardless of type, the drier and smaller the logs, the quicker your fire will light and burn.

WOODSTOVES

When you burn a fire in a fireplace, about three-quarters of the heat is wasted up the chimney. When you burn a fire in a woodstove, more than three-quarters of the heat stays in the room. This difference has a huge bearing on how many logs you need to burn in each type of fire and therefore how expensive, relatively, they are to run.

For those deciding whether to buy a woodstove, however, the economics are slightly more complex, as you'll need to factor in the cost of a stove and professional installation. Estimates suggest that the payback period is between five and ten years, depending on how much you use the stove.

Woodstoves also combust wood in a different way than fireplaces do—modern woodstoves recirculate air through the stove, which not only makes them combust more efficiently but also means that most of the harmful particulates and gases burn off before they reach the chimney. Many homes in towns and cities are within smoke-control areas, where you can't emit smoke from a chimney unless you're burning an authorized fuel or using an exempt appliance. Most modern woodstoves are classed as exempt.

One thing the fireplace has over the woodstove, however, is the sensory experience. Tucked behind a glass door, a stove fire is safer and less smoky but also silent and removed. Woodstoves don't work well with their doors open, so if you want a fire for its delightful crackle, or for toasting marshmallows or making scented smoke, best to stick to the traditional hearth.

BANKING UP

Some people recommend stuffing your woodstove with enough fuel to keep it going through the night until morning. This is called "banking up," and while this idea sounds good in principle—how cozy to wake up to a still-glowing fire—in practice it's actually bad news for your woodstove, and potentially very dangerous.

Modern woodstoves are designed to burn efficiently by operating at a high temperature, with plenty of airflow and properly seasoned logs. All the methods people use to bank up their woodstove at night affect the efficiency of this combustion. One traditional trick, for example, is to light unseasoned logs, the idea being that the wet wood burns at a low, smoldering temperature for longer. This might make the fire last a few more hours, but it leads to condensation and other acidic residues that can damage your flue and the inside of the stove.

Other techniques, like restricting the airflow or filling the stove to the brim, result in the fire not being able to get hot enough to combust fully—not a good idea, especially when it can result in the production of the lethal gas carbon monoxide.

One absolute no-no is adding coal. While you can buy multi-fuel stoves (see Coal, page 62), woodstoves are designed to burn timber exclusively.

Wood burns best on a flat bed of ash, whereas coal needs to sit on a raised grate to allow extra airflow. Burning coal and wood together in a woodstove will mean neither combusts properly, leaving sulfuric acid deposits to corrode your flue, and you run the risk of damaging your stove or, even worse, causing a flue gas explosion in the stove or chimney.

CHIMNEYS

If a fire is the heart of the house, the chimney is the lungs. Its sole purpose in life is to help the air in your home stay breathable and allow harmful flue gases to escape up and out of your home.

If you are new to a property and don't know whether the chimney works, *don't use it* until it's been smoke-tested and swept (see Sweeps, page 142). Even if you know the fireplace works, if you are putting an old chimney back into use after a long period of disuse, it'll need testing and sweeping. Chimneys have a habit of getting blocked by nests, animals, debris, and smoky residues, all of which can restrict airflow or cause a chimney fire.

If you're fitting a woodstove into an existing chimney, it will need a metal flue liner. This is for three reasons: wood burns at a lower temperature than coal, and therefore harmful deposits such as tar are more likely to stick to the inside of the chimney; a metal liner will stop noxious fumes such as carbon monoxide from leaking into upstairs rooms; and a metal liner keeps the flue gases warmer for longer, helping them rise up and out of the chimney. The stove manufacturer can tell you the specific size you need.

If your property does not have a chimney, you can have an insulated metal flue installed. These can look handsomely architectural and, because they are lined, aren't dangerously hot to the touch.

AIR

If you try to burn a fire where there's not enough oxygen—in a sealed room, for example—instead of creating carbon dioxide, you get carbon monoxide, an odorless, colorless gas that can be fatal. If you want a wood fire in your home, whether it's in a fireplace or a woodstove, you must ensure there's a constant supply of fresh air.

In the past, homes were so drafty that fireplaces had a ready supply of oxygen, whether it came from leaky windows or howling floorboards. Fresh air could be drawn from both outside the home and other rooms inside, helping the fire burn efficiently. In modern homes, which are better insulated, many of these sources of air are blocked or sealed.

It's not practical to have a window open all the time, especially when you're trying to keep warm which is why any fireplaces that take their combustion air from within the home must have a ventilator that is permanently fixed open to provide fresh air from outside. It's not a difficult job to fit one, and it's absolutely essential—not only is it often a legal requirement, but it's also a lifesaver.

If you're planning on buying a woodstove, consult local, state, and federal regulations (see Resources, page 156) for guidance on ventilation.

HOW TO PUT OUT A FIRE

If you're preparing to put out your fire, stop adding fuel about an hour before you want the fire to die. If your fire is in a woodstove, simply make sure the glass door is tightly closed and the primary air vent is shut (this is usually the vent at the bottom of the stove). The secondary air vent stays open—this allows the stove to keep burning at a safe level of combustion while slowly dying out. Never throw water on a woodstove; it could crack the cast metal.

If your fire is in a fireplace, kill it in two stages:

STAGE ONE: Take a poker and "open up" the fire by separating any burning logs. Gently spread out the embers; this will cool the fire.

STAGE TWO: Use a spray bottle to lightly spritz the flames with water. Don't flood the fire; it makes the ashes sticky and fills the room with smoke. A sprinkling of sand or cold ashes will do the same trick (you'll need to clear out the sand before you make a new fire). Even if the fire looks dead, ALWAYS put a fireguard up before you leave the room—it only takes one stray spark to wreak havoc.

To put out a campfire, follow the same principle. Use a stick or metal shovel to separate the logs and flatten out the embers. Pour water over the hot ashes until the hissing stops. If you don't have any water, stir soil or sand into the embers to smother the flames. Never bury a fire; it can smolder for hours.

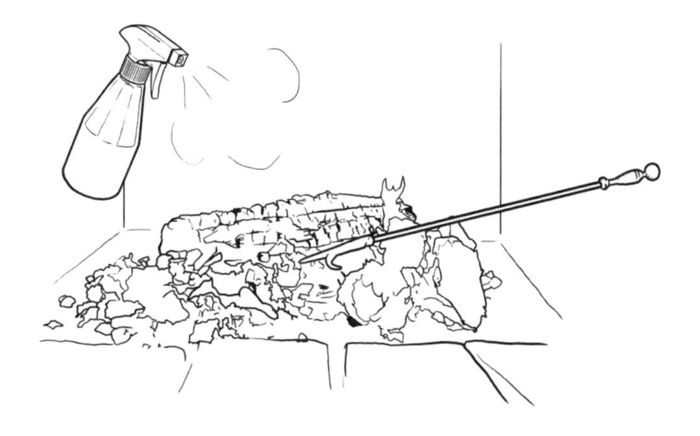

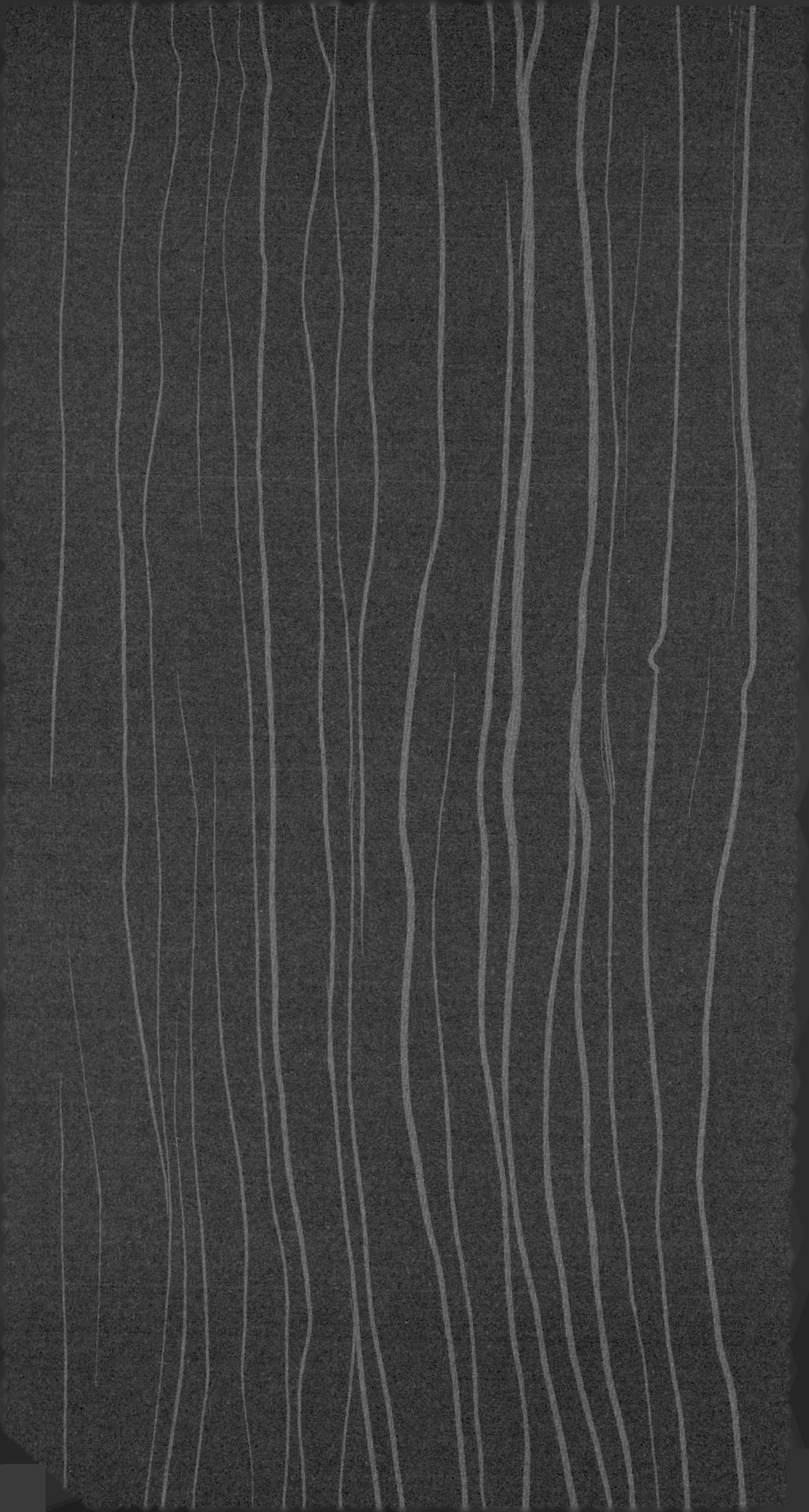

CHAPTER THREE

Choosing Firewood

Beechwood fires burn bright and clear,
    Hornbeam blazes too,
If the logs are kept a year,
    to season through and through.
Oaken logs will warm you well,
    if they're old and dry,
Larch logs of pinewood smell
    but the sparks will fly.
Pine is good and so is Yew for
    warmth through wintry days,
The Poplar and the Willow too,
    they take too long to blaze.
Birch logs will burn too fast,
    Alder scarce at all,
Chestnut logs are good to last,
    cut them in the fall.
Holly logs will burn like wax,
    you should burn them green,
Elm logs like smouldering flax,
    no flames with them are seen.
Pear logs and Apple logs,
    they will scent your room,
Cherry logs, across the dogs,
    they smell like flowers in bloom.
Ash logs, so smooth and grey,
    burn them green or old,
Buy up all that come your way,
    they're worth their weight in gold.

—OLD ENGLISH FOLK SONG

BURNING HARDWOOD VS. SOFTWOOD

All wood burns, but some woods burn better than others. When you're choosing firewood, it's helpful to divide timber into two categories—hardwood and softwood. The names don't refer to the texture of the wood—some hardwoods are soft and vice versa.

Softwoods come from conifer trees, which are evergreen, needle-leaved, and have cones, like fir and pine.

Hardwoods come from broad-leaved deciduous trees—species like oak, elm, ash, and cherry fall into this category.

As a general rule, hardwoods are denser than softwoods, so they provide a longer burn. They also have less resin than softwoods, so they are not as prone to clog up your chimney with tar. Hardwood is, however, more difficult to ignite, so you'll find that most kindling is made from softwood.

You can burn a fire entirely with softwood, but because it doesn't last as long as hardwood, you'll find yourself throwing on logs at an alarming rate. Softwood also tends to spit and smoke, which can be tricky if you're building a fire in a fireplace.

Softwood does have the advantage of being cheaper than hardwood—this is because it seasons more quickly (see Seasoning, page 76), it's readily available, and you get less heat output per log than with hardwood.

If possible, the best solution is to burn a mix of the two. Softwood will bring heat quickly and cheaply, while hardwood burns slow and long. Think of softwood as the sprinter fuel and hardwood as the distance runner.

It's worth noting that woodstoves are less fussy about which wood will burn because the combustion process is so efficient. That said, the more softwood you burn in a woodstove, the more often you'll need to have your chimney swept.

WOOD THAT'S NO GOOD

Just because you can set fire to something doesn't mean you should. Here's what not to burn:

TREATED TIMBER—Preservatives, fungicides, creosote, paints, glues, varnishes, and other chemical additives can release highly toxic fumes and will damage your chimney. Steer clear of burning MDF (medium-density fiberboard); chipboard; plywood;

decking; stained, pressure-treated, or painted timber; and anything treated for outdoor use.

SOLUTION: *Recycle it instead.*

NON-LOCAL TIMBER—Never move firewood long distances. Transporting logs can spread invasive species, tree pests, and fungi that lead to blights that threaten woodland and native species.

SOLUTION: *Buy it where you burn it.*

GREEN TIMBER—Unless it's an emergency, avoid burning wet or unseasoned wood. It's hard to light, burns inefficiently, pollutes the atmosphere with particulates, and clogs up your chimney.

SOLUTION: *Season your wood properly before burning (see Seasoning, page 76)*

POISONOUS TIMBER—There's little research into tree species and toxic smoke, so local knowledge and folklore are often all we have to rely on. Traditionally, oleander, poison ivy, poison oak, and sumac are cited as being poisonous to inhale, so be sure to avoid those species when you're building your fire.

SOLUTION: *Only burn timber listed in the Timber Table (see page 152).*

DRIFTWOOD—While it burns well, salt-laden driftwood produces smoke that can speed the corrosion of metal stoves and flue parts. Recent research also suggests that burning sodium chloride releases toxic dioxins at high temperatures.

SOLUTION: *Avoid if possible.*

BUYING FIREWOOD

If you want to find a reputable, fairly priced supply of firewood, be sure to consider the following:

VOLUME, NOT WEIGHT—Buy wood by volume, *not* weight; that way you won't be cheated with heavy, unseasoned logs. Ask what you are getting in cubic feet or meters—suppliers often sell by the trailer load or bundle, but they need to clarify what that equates to in volume. If they won't tell you, go elsewhere. You wouldn't order other heating fuels without knowing exactly how much you were getting.

SOFTWOOD OR HARDWOOD—Hardwood costs more for the same volume of softwood but will last longer in your fire. If possible, consider buying a mix of the two.

GREEN OR SEASONED—You can buy green (freshly cut), part-seasoned, or fully seasoned logs. Green is cheapest, but you will have to season it yourself before you burn it. If you have the storage space and time, buying green can be cost-efficient. If you want to burn the wood now, buy fully seasoned. Consider investing in a moisture meter so you can check any deliveries (see Moisture Meters, page 78). Kiln-dried logs (see page 60) are another alternative.

SUSTAINABLE SOURCES—Only buy firewood from a sustainable, ethical source. Foreign imports of logs have heavy carbon footprints, and it can be difficult to find out whether the producer is committed to responsible, sustainable woodland management. Look for quality assurances or buy from a locally managed estate.

SALVAGE

A vast amount of wood is sent to landfill each year, much of it burnable. One of the issues is knowing what's safe to burn and what's best to skip. Anything that's engineered, laminated, treated, or painted will contain glues, formaldehyde, fungicides, or other chemicals that are harmful to humans if burned. Most scrap is softwood, so it's best kept for kindling or to mix with hardwood in a fireplace. A woodstove will cope admirably with softwood, but remember, you'll need to sweep your chimney more often.

SCAVENGING

It's trickier to scavenge wood than you might think. Most woodland is privately owned and managed, whether by a forestry organization or a landowner, and the trees—alive or dead—are their property. Taking wood to burn without permission is effectively theft. That said, there are ways of collecting wood in the wild:

SCAVENGING PERMITS—Many National Forests and Bureau of Land Management (BLM) areas allow you to collect firewood for personal use, but you must first obtain a Forest Service–issued permit. You must have the permit with you when you're in the forest. To learn more about Forest Service permits, contact the local National Forest or BLM office.

LOCAL LANDOWNERS—Some woodland owners may be happy for you to remove deadwood or take part in thinning or coppicing days in return for a portion of the rewards. It's worth starting a dialogue with the local landowner to see whether there's any labor you could volunteer in return for firewood.

GROW YOUR OWN—If you have land, there may be grants and funding available to help you create your own copse or woodland. Even a largish garden can support enough trees for a modest firewood supply—choose quick-growing hardwood varieties that produce good-quality firewood, such as alder, ash, hawthorn, and sycamore.

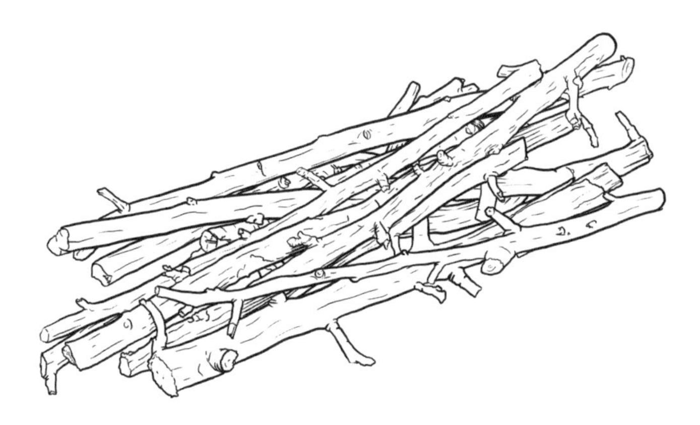

GOOD TO BURN VS. SKIP IT

GOOD TO BURN

Wooden pallets, cable drums, and crates (don't burn if stamped "MB," as this means it has been treated with methyl bromide, a fumigant; "HB" means it was heat-treated, so it is fine to burn).

Untreated framing and studwork timber

Planed softwood and hardwood

Solid wood flooring and skirting boards (unvarnished and unpainted)

Scaffold boards (untreated)

Thermowood

Untreated shiplap or tongue and groove

Roofing trusses

SKIP IT

Sheet materials (chipboard, melamine, veneers, hardboard, plywood, MDF, particleboard)

Laminate and engineered flooring

Painted or varnished wood

Outdoor timber (decking, cladding, cedar shingles, site pegs, gates, fences, and posts)

Salvaged telephone poles

Roofing batten board

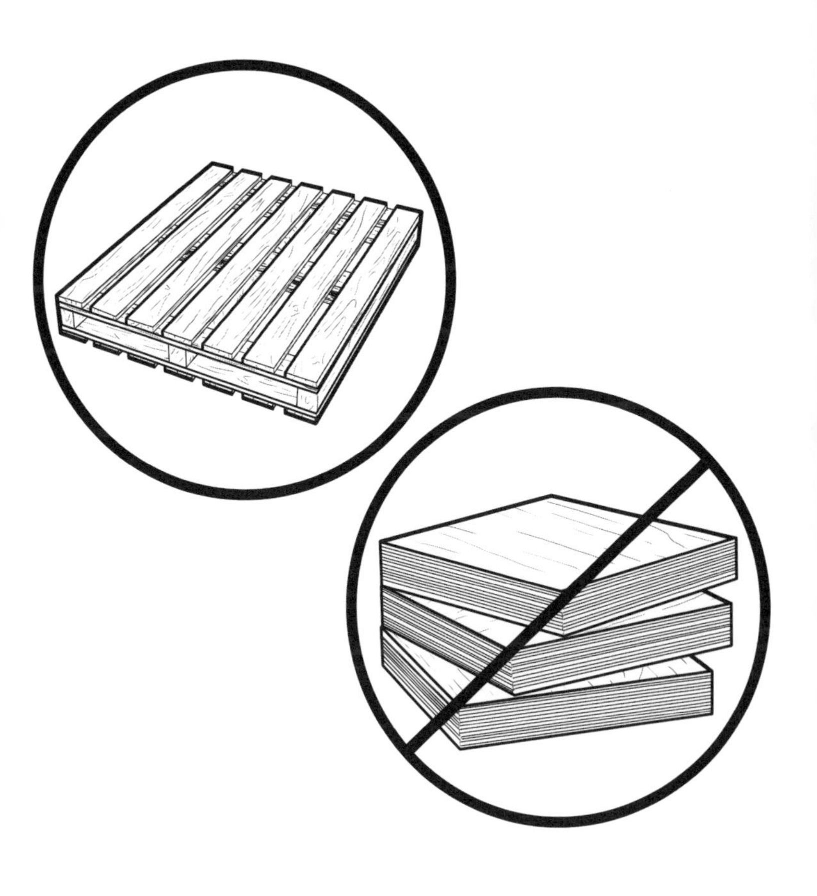

KILN-DRIED LOGS

For a fire to burn effectively and cleanly, logs need to be no more than 25 percent water, and ideally less than that (see Seasoning, page 76). The traditional way to get to this point is to dry, or "season," your wood for a long period of time (how long depends on the species). If you need dry wood in a hurry, you can pay a premium and buy kiln-dried logs.

As the name suggests, logs are "cooked" in a large kiln to speed the drying process. In many cases, kiln-dried logs are actually drier than seasoned logs (typically between 10 percent and 20 percent water), which makes them popular for a number of reasons. The lack of moisture means a cleaner, hotter burn than traditionally seasoned logs, so fewer kiln-dried logs give the same heat output, which may help offset the higher price. The hotter burn also creates fewer particulates, which is good news for air quality and your chimney.

Whether kiln-dried logs are always better for the environment is difficult to calculate, as the kilns require fuel. And many kiln-dried logs travel large distances, adding to their carbon footprint, and may come from forests that aren't sustainably managed. If you can find a supplier who uses waste wood, renewable energy, or biomass to heat their kilns and sources their wood from local, managed woodland, you've got the best of both worlds.

FIRELOGS

What looks like a log, burns like a log, but isn't a log?

FIRELOGS—Created from compressed sawdust, firelogs—like Duraflame—have the benefit of burning hotter and cleaner than traditional logs and taking up half the space. They also score eco-points for using up a waste product of the timber industry. Firelogs don't have quite the same aesthetic appeal of logs, nor the fragrant smoke, but if you're using a woodstove this doesn't matter so much.

DIY PAPER LOGS—Making paper logs may seem like a handy way of using up old newspapers, but it's not so good for your chimney or local air quality. While black ink burns fairly cleanly, colored ink, which is used in most newspapers, produces noxious fumes and particulates that contribute to air pollution and flue damage.

CHARCOAL—*Never* use charcoal in an indoor fireplace or woodstove. It releases significant amounts of poisonous carbon monoxide (even after it starts to cool down). Charcoal also burns too hot for a woodstove.

COAL

Burning wood and coal together can be problematic for a variety of reasons. Consider the following before using coal in your next fire:

WOOD AND COAL BURN DIFFERENTLY—Wood needs to burn on a flat surface with an air supply from above. Coal needs air from *underneath*, so sits on a raised grate. The grate also allows coal ash to escape without blocking the air supply. While wood and coal will burn together, you won't be getting the maximum efficiency from either.

WOOD AND COAL CREATE SULFURIC ACID—Burning wood and coal together risks causing serious damage to your chimney or flue. Wood contains water. Coal contains sulfur. Burn them simultaneously and you create sulfuric acid, which is corrosive and could shorten the life of your stove or chimney. Using a handful of seasoned kindling to start a coal fire isn't an issue; it's burning the two fuels together over a prolonged period that can cause problems.

COAL WILL KILL YOUR WOODSTOVE—Coal burns at a much hotter temperature than timber does. The materials used to make many woodstoves are simply not designed to take repeated and long-standing exposure to extreme temperatures and may warp or crack.

MULTI-FUEL STOVES—Multi-fuel stoves are designed to be able to adapt to different types of fuel, either by including a removable grate or having different options for air supply. If you want to switch between fuels, these can be a good option, but most manufacturers will still recommend that you don't mix fuels in the same fire.

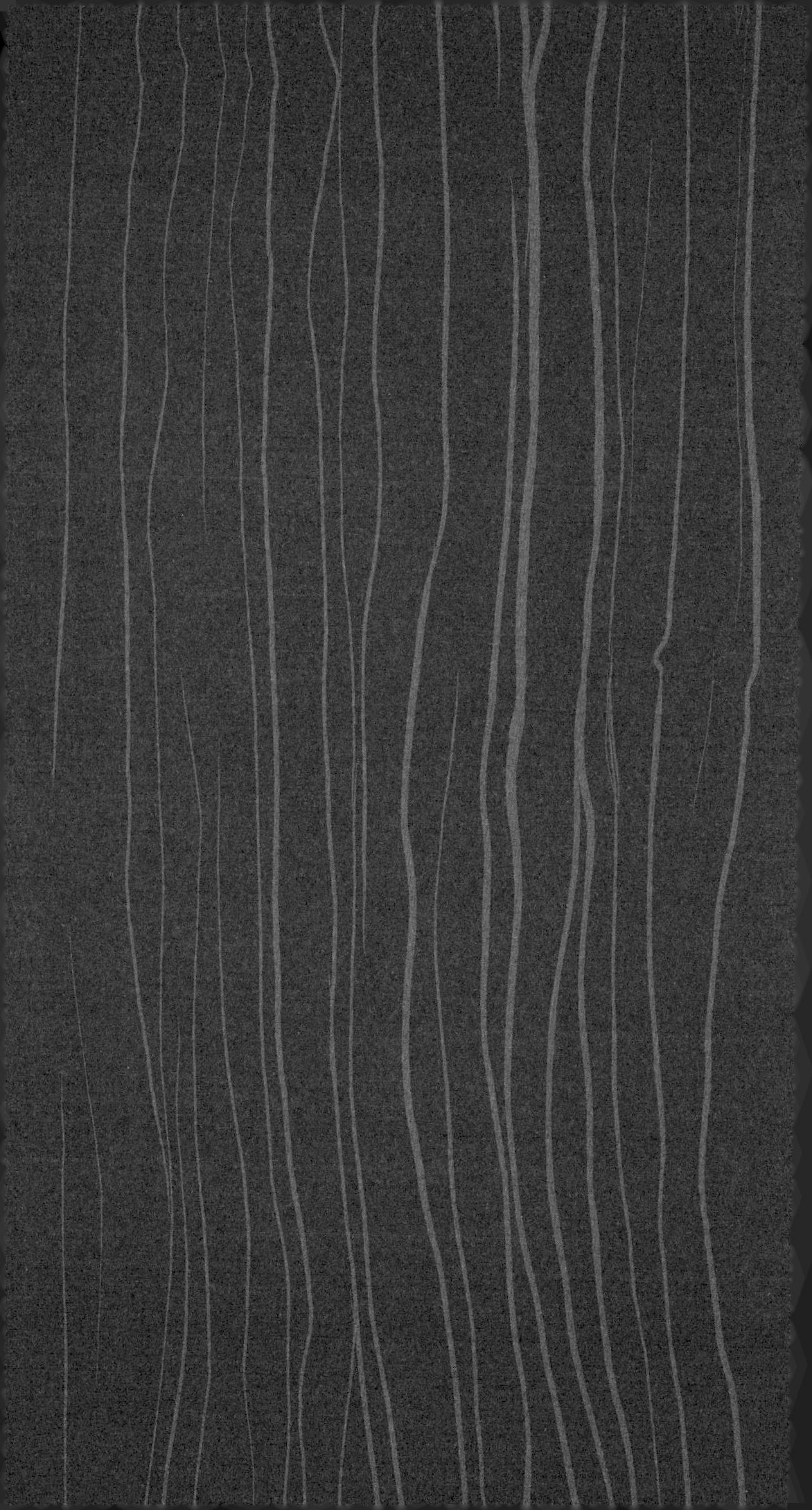

CHAPTER FOUR

Chop, Stack, Store

To love is to burn, to be on fire.

—JANE AUSTEN, *SENSE AND SENSIBILITY*

GREEN WOOD

When you cut down a tree, the freshly felled wood is about 50 percent moisture. That means every unseasoned log you throw on a fire is half timber, half water. A fire must drive off this water before it can start to kick out any decent heat, so by using wet wood you are radically slowing down the rate at which your room will warm up.

If a fire burns too coolly, it also doesn't burn as cleanly. Setting fire to unseasoned wood means that harmful particulates and gases don't burn off before they reach the chimney—not great for the environment or your air quality. Green wood can also cause creosote to build up on the inside of your chimney, which is one of the leading causes of chimney fires.

So, whether you are using a fireplace or a woodstove, all firewood should be seasoned properly before you burn it (see Seasoning, page 76). Green wood will sizzle, hiss, or even bubble on the fire and produce lots of smoldering smoke, rather than a hot, clean flame. You can also tell if wood is green from its weight—wet wood is heavier than the equivalent seasoned log.

On a camping trip, if you don't have any alternative, there are a few tree species that you can burn green. Ash, birch, holly, and sycamore will all burn green.

CHOPPING BLOCKS

While some people choose to split wood directly on the ground, there are good reasons to use a block. First, it's safer—you want the axe to land well away from your feet; second, it's easier on your back—you don't have to bring the axe down beyond knee height; and finally, it reduces the chances of your axe being damaged through hitting the ground or bouncing off any stray rocks. Consider the following when choosing your chopping spot:

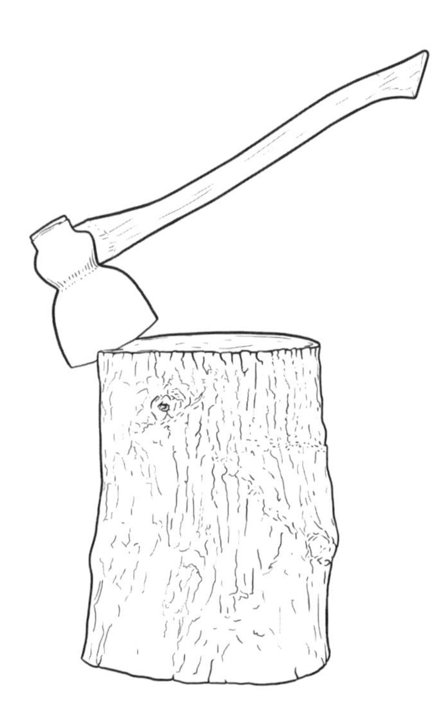

- Find somewhere well away from windows, animals, and other people, and give yourself plenty of room to swing the axe.
- If possible, split the logs next to where you plan to stack them to avoid having to carry your pile several times.
- Always set your block to face the approach—you don't want people walking up behind you unheard or unseen.
- Find a good chopping block. A cut tree stump or section of trunk is ideal. You can find chopping blocks online if you can't source one locally.
- Choose a block that is wide, heavy, flat on both ends, and right for your height—the axe should strike the end of the log at a right angle. Most people find a comfortable height and width is about 14 by 14 inches (35 by 35 centimeters).
- Sit the block on solid, stable ground. If you place a chopping block on a soft surface such as a lawn, you'll find much of the energy is absorbed into the ground.
- The block must be absolutely stable. If it's wobbly, a glancing blow could hit your lower body or send the timber flying off.

SPLITTING WOOD

1. **CHOOSE YOUR WEAPON.** You'll need a splitting axe or a maul (a cross between a heavy axe and a sledgehammer). For most small logs, a splitting axe works just fine.
2. **WEAR THE RIGHT CLOTHES.** Wear safety glasses, gloves to prevent blisters, and solid work boots (preferably steel toed).
3. **STAND CORRECTLY.** Stand squarely facing your chopping block, feet shoulder-width apart. Don't stand with one leg in front of the other—if you're standing incorrectly and miss the target, your front leg is the first place an axe will land.
4. **CHOOSE YOUR LOG.** You need straight sections of timber that will balance upright when placed on the chopping block. Don't attempt to split curved logs or logs with large knots—you'll be endlessly thwarted.
5. **READ THE WOOD.** Exploit any existing cracks or splits. If you can't find any, aim for the center.
6. **HOLD THE AXE PROPERLY.** Hold the base of the handle in one hand (most people prefer their left hand). Slide your right hand up the shaft to near the head of the axe.
7. **SWING IN ONE MOTION.** In a single fluid action, raise the axe over your shoulder. Letting the weight of the axe do the work, bring

the axe down onto the log, letting your right hand slide down the shaft to meet the left.

8. **LET THE AXE DO THE WORK.** Allow the momentum and sheer weight of the axe to provide the power, not your own brute force. You are simply guiding the axe to where it needs to fall.

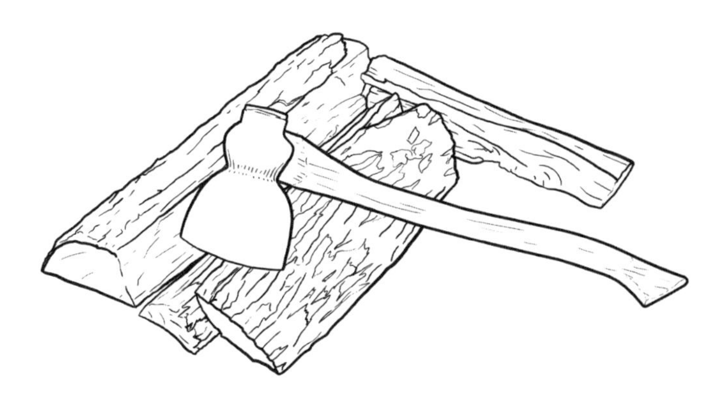

THE PERFECT LOG STORE

A log store is a storage device for drying wood. A log store should do two things: help the seasoning process, and protect your firewood from the elements. If you want to build or buy a log store, keep the following in mind:

BREATHABILITY—Your stack must allow air to circulate. This helps the logs dry out so they're ready for burning. Most log stores have slatted or open sides.

AIRFLOW—Air needs to flow underneath the log store, so the base should be slightly raised off the ground (on feet or bearers). A gravel or paved surface is better than grass or soil.

STABILITY—A sizable stack of logs will exert significant pressure on the sides and base of your log store. The ground needs to be firm and level to support the log store and provide stability.

WEATHER—Try not to site your log store where it will catch the bad weather. A sunny, airy spot that isn't vulnerable to driving rain is ideal.

WALLS—If you want to put your logs next to a wall, leave an air gap of 2 inches (5 centimeters). This breathing room aids the drying process.

MATERIALS—Most timber won't hold up to weather without treatment. Buy outdoor-grade timber or species that naturally resist decay, such as oak and cedar. Any nails or fasteners need to be rust-resistant.

SIZE—Estimate how many cubic feet or meters of logs you'll need a year (see Fire and Cost, page 28) and aim to stack a year's worth. If you want to season your own green wood (see Seasoning, page 76), ideally you should have three separate stores or areas—one for fully seasoned (two years old), one for part-seasoned (one year), and one for green (this year's).

HOW TO STACK LOGS

Few things are more pleasing than a neatly stacked log pile. It's not just a thing of beauty; it's also the larder for your fire, so you need to be able to grab the right mix of ingredients in one go.

LOGS SHOULD BE UNIFORM LENGTHS—Cut or buy the right size log for your fire or woodstove—usually around 12 inches (30 centimeters).

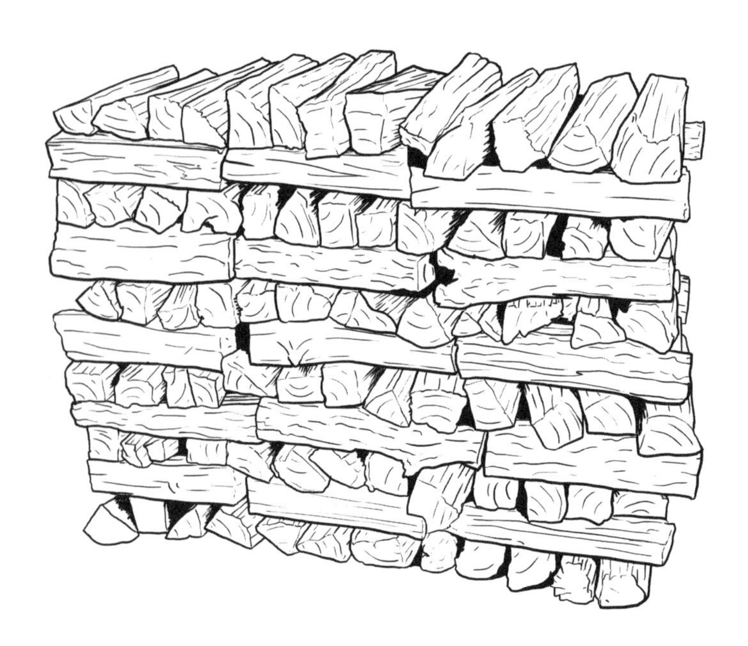

DON'T HAVE LOGS TOO CHUNKY—Wood should be split to a variety of sizes, ranging from 3 to 6 inches (7 to 15 centimeters) at its widest point.

SPLIT IS ALWAYS BEST—The extra surface area speeds the seasoning process.

THINK IN HORIZONTAL LINES—Plan to stack and remove logs in lines, rather than working randomly through the pile.

MIX SIZES ACROSS THE LINES—You'll use a variety of different-size logs in the course of a fire, so stack each horizontal line with a mix of large and small logs.

DON'T TRY AND PACK TOO TIGHTLY—Build in air gaps to help the drying process; mixing up the sizes of logs helps with this.

PLACE BARK UPWARD—Logs should be stacked bark side up because this will help the firewood shed any moisture that comes in from above.

KEEP IT STABLE—Don't take logs from the middle or bottom of the pile; it'll destabilize the stack. If you want to stack more than one log deep, use a double-length log to bridge both stacks and create a "tie" between the two.

KEEP KINDLING SEPARATE—A large bin or box is ideal for kindling, which just needs to be kept dry and easily accessible.

SEASONING

Seasoned wood burns hotter, cleaner, and greener than wet wood does. But different trees take different lengths of time to dry out, and different thicknesses of wood season at different rates. Use the following list to determine when your logs are ready to burn (not all of the following apply to every species, so use a combination of checks to be sure):

CRACKS—Look for radial cracks and splits on the log, the more the better.

COLOR—Seasoned wood loses its vibrant color. Choose faded, pale, and gray logs.

CHIPS—Bark should fall off easily; the drier the wood, the looser the bark.

SPLINTERS—Dry wood will be prone to splintering.

SMELL—Wet wood smells strongly of sap; dry wood has a delicate, woody aroma.

SOUND—Knock two pieces together. You want a hollow clunk rather than a dull thud.

FOR ACCURACY, USE A MOISTURE METER—These devices can give you an indication of the percentage of water in your firewood (see Moisture Meters, page 78) and work best if you test a sample of logs from any one load. Aim for 20 percent, and don't burn anything higher than 25 percent.

DIFFERENT SPECIES TAKE DIFFERENT TIMES TO SEASON—Dense hardwoods like oak, beech, and hornbeam may take two years to fully season, while conifers and fast-growing broadleaves like ash and birch can be ready in a year (see the Timber Table for suggested seasoning times, page 152).

WHICHEVER VARIETY YOU CHOOSE, YOU CAN SPEED THE DRYING PROCESS IN THREE WAYS—More heat, greater airflow, and smaller log size. Keep narrower logs in a warm, dry, well-ventilated place (like an open-sided shed or lean-to) and your firewood seasoning times drop dramatically.

DOUBLE-DRYING

Timber is like a sponge. It can both absorb and release water, depending on how much moisture is in the air around it. In most outdoor conditions, seasoned firewood will never be drier than around 12 to 18 percent moisture content.

But indoor air is often drier than this. Thanks to central heating and better insulation, during the winter months the air in the average home contains much less moisture than outside (which is why some of us get dry skin). We can use this to our advantage and bring seasoned wood indoors for a last blast of extra drying.

Which raises the question—why don't you dry all green wood indoors? In theory you could, but you'd need plenty of air movement, heat, and space, which is just not practical for most of us. Also, the moisture from the green timber has to go somewhere—you don't want that amount of extra moisture indoors, where it can cause damp, mold, and other issues.

Stick to seasoned wood, and view double-drying as an extra measure. Simply bring in your seasoned wood and store it near your heat source (but not too near—see Staying Safe Indoors, page 116) or a radiator, in a container that allows air movement (a large wicker basket is ideal). Even if it's just for a few days, it all helps.

NOTE: *Some woodstoves have metal log stores underneath, but don't be tempted to stack logs against the sides of the stove—that would create a serious fire hazard.*

MOISTURE METERS

If you want to test how dry your logs are, invest in a moisture meter. These simple, handheld devices tell you in seconds whether the firewood you've just had delivered is properly seasoned, or it can give you an accurate idea of how much further your log stack has to dry.

Most moisture meters have two sharp prongs on the end, which you press into the piece of timber you're testing. The meter uses a low electrical current to test the proportion of water to wood in any given sample. Sounds easy, but logs have a habit of giving off unreliable readings, especially if you test the outside of a crateful or the dry ėnd of damp log.

The wettest part of any log will be at its heart, so you'll need to split any wood you are testing. Just prodding the end or pre-split surface (which dries out more quickly) will give you a false reading. Similarly, if you have a well-seasoned crate of logs that's just been rained on, testing the outer surfaces would give too wet a reading.

As with any good experiment, run your test more than once by checking several logs. A mix of samples from inside and outside the stack or crate will help even out any huge variations. You should also test in more than one spot on the same log and average the results. Remember—you want a reading of around 20 percent or less, and certainly no more than 25 percent.

LOG BASKETS

You need to get your fuel from the log store to the fire. And you also need somewhere to store timber by the fireside. There are lots of different options for log carriers, from log holders to baskets, iron frames, or log bags; ultimately, it comes down to practicality and preference.

One of the problems is that anything big enough to hold a decent amount of logs is often very heavy to carry. And if you use the same basket to both transport logs and store them by the fire, you will likely leave a trail of bark and debris in your wake. The best solution is to have a combination of static baskets and portable log carriers. That way, you can dash out to the log store and grab a manageable amount of timber in one go, without having to disrupt your fireside arrangement.

KINDLING BUCKET—Have a small bucket or basket by the fireside, primed with small, dry pieces. Even better if it has a handle so you can fill it up outside and bring it in.

LOG BASKET—Choose a large, sturdy basket or wooden crate that's robust enough to take logs being dumped into it from a height. If you've got room for two baskets, even better; that way you can double-dry them.

LOG CARRIER—Fetching logs in by the armful is fine, but it might damage your clothes. Canvas log bags will carry a sizable load and fold away when you don't need them. Look for strong handles and wipeable fabric.

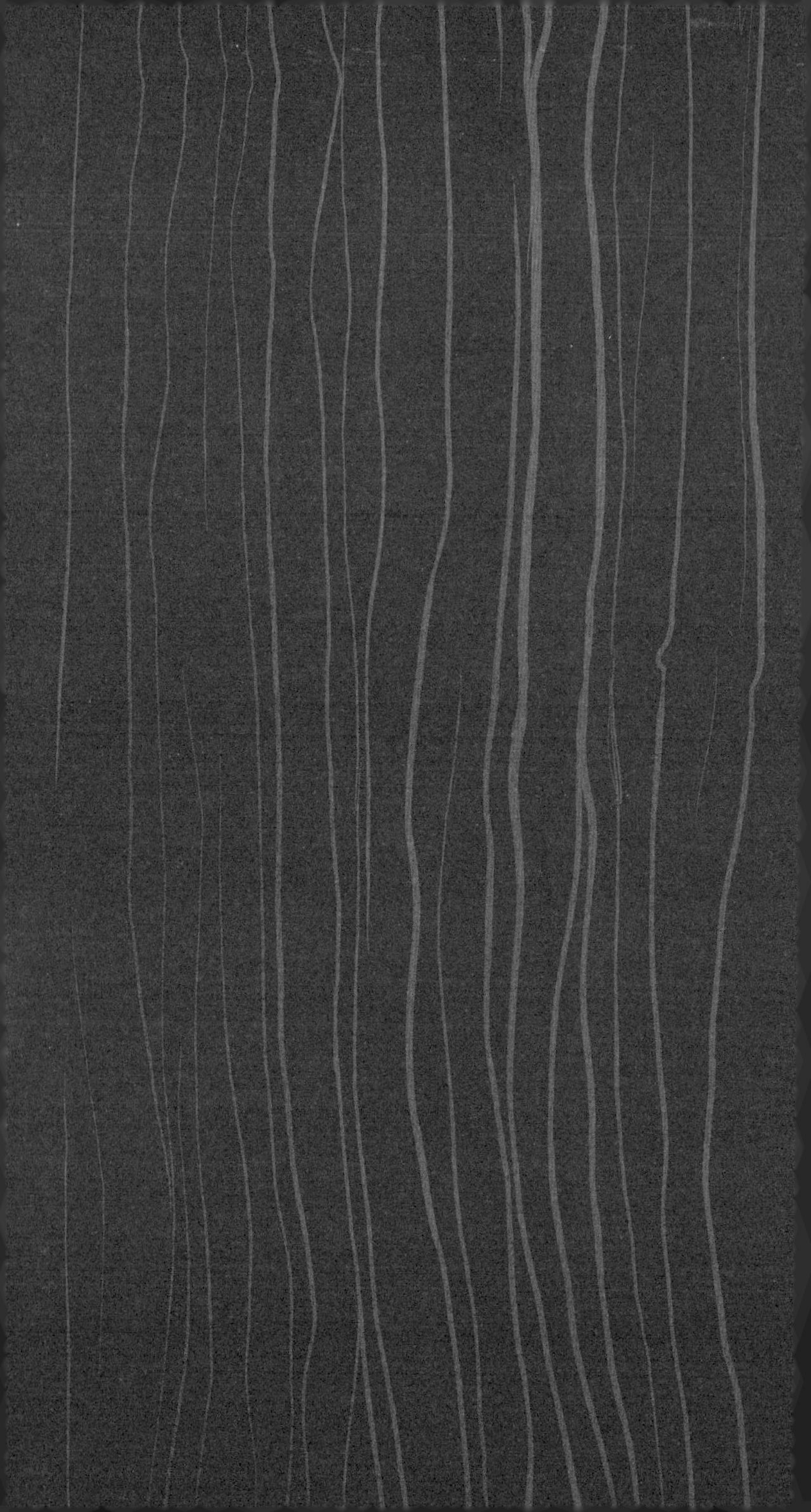

CHAPTER FIVE

Starting a Fire

Education is not the filling of a pail, but the lighting of a fire.

—W. B. YEATS

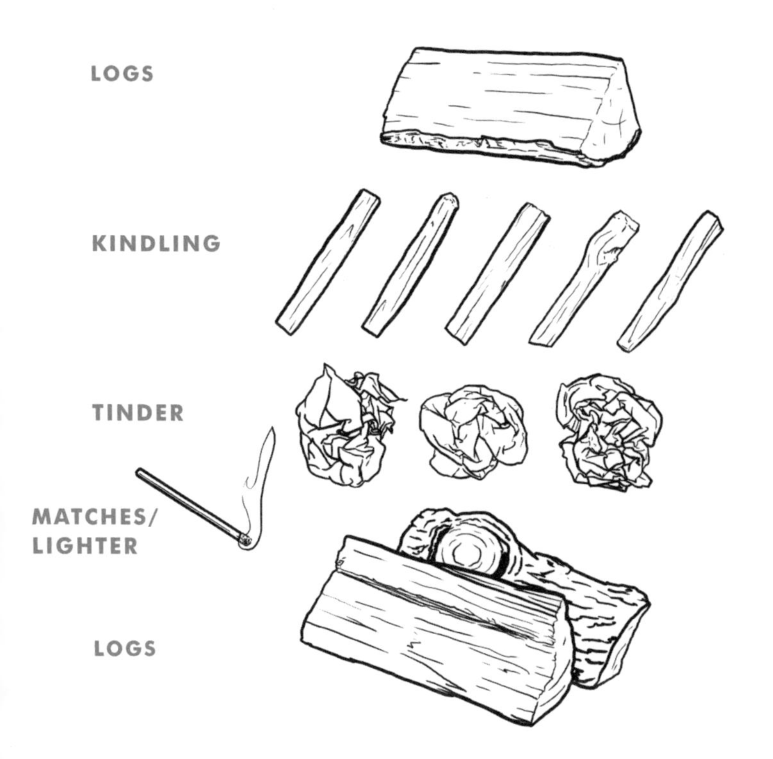
LOGS
KINDLING
TINDER
MATCHES/
LIGHTER
LOGS

THE YOUNG FIRE

The first five or ten minutes of a fire are the most crucial and, potentially, the most frustrating. It's a process that can't be rushed, involving a sequence that allows the fire to grow in stages. In this chapter, you'll find lots of different ways to construct the perfect fire, but here are a few important things to check before you even light the paper:

» **OPEN THE AIR SUPPLY.** Whether it's opening the damper or pulling out the air vent on a woodstove, don't forget your fire needs plenty of oxygen.

» **HAVE YOUR TINDER OR FIRELIGHTERS READY.** Make sure you've already got plenty of newspaper crumpled into balls, your tinder heaped in a mound, or your firelighters (see Firelighters, page 88) ready.

» **DON'T SCRIMP ON KINDLING.** Use handfuls of very dry, thin kindling at this stage, and make sure there's space between the kindling to let air circulate.

» **BE PATIENT.** Don't try to do everything at once, unless you're making a top-down fire (see The Top-Down Fire, page 108); put too much timber, or logs that are too wide, on the fire to begin with and you might smother the flames.

» **MAINTAIN THE HEAT.** Pay attention to how your fire is catching. If the fire looks as though it's struggling, add smaller logs to raise the temperature. If it's burning too fast and flames are roaring up the chimney, add a larger log to bring the heat down. The aim is to have plenty of glowing heat without too many flames. You'll soon get a feel for it.

FIRELIGHTERS

Traditionally, you start a fire with tinder and a flame. The flame ignites the tinder, the tinder ignites the kindling, and the kindling ignites the logs. But finding suitable, dry tinder isn't always easy, so firelighters are a reliable, quick alternative and cut out one stage of the fire-building process if you're in a hurry.

The downside is that most commercial firelighter cubes contain a number of either polluting or toxic ingredients, such as kerosene or urea-formaldehyde. They are also poisonous if ingested—not ideal if you have small children or pets around. Always keep firelighters out of reach of little hands and paws.

The good news is there's an increasing movement toward eco-friendly firelighters, made from a whole host of flammable, nontoxic ingredients, such as vegetable oils, beeswax, wood shavings, sawdust, and wood chips. Not only are they less polluting, but they also tend to be odor free, which makes them useful if you are lighting a cooking fire (see The Cowboy Fire, page 112).

Liquid firelighters are only designed for outdoor use, such as bonfires and campfires, and are *not* suitable for indoor fireplaces and woodstoves. Not only do they release vapors that are toxic if inhaled, but they are also potentially explosive. You should also never use liquid firelighters to "refresh" a fire—whether indoors or out—as the fumes can ignite and cause severe burns. Only use liquid firelighter on an unlit fire, allowing the liquid to soak into the kindling before lighting it with a long safety match. The safest brands of liquid firelighter have child-resistant caps and anti-flashback nozzles.

NOTE: *NEVER use an accelerant to light a fire. Gas and liquid paraffin both give off powerful vapors. When you pour an accelerant onto a fire, the flames can follow the vapors back and up to the source—that is, you or the gas can in your hand.*

HOMEMADE FIRELIGHTERS

If you want to make your own firelighters, here's an easy recipe. You can use traditional candle wax, soy wax, or beeswax (soy wax and beeswax are non-petroleum-based, making them better for the environment and indoor air quality). The optional addition of a few drops of essential oil means you can add spicy, wintery notes, such as sandalwood, cinnamon, and nutmeg. Homemade firelighters also make really pretty gifts.

YOU'LL NEED:

- Cupcake tin
- Paper cupcake liners
- Pack of tealights (soy or beeswax if possible)
- A few drops of your favorite essential oils (optional)
- Tweezers
- Dry pinecones

INSTRUCTIONS:

1. Line the cupcake tin with the paper liners.
2. Remove the tealights from their metal tins and place one in each liner.

3. In a moderate oven, melt the wax until it is liquid and the wick is floating.
4. Take out of the oven and add a few drops of essential oil to each mold, if desired.
5. With tweezers, move the wick to the edge of paper liner and sit a pinecone upright in the melted wax. Make sure the wick is still accessible.
6. When completely cool, peel away the paper liner.
7. You can also add spices or herbal sprigs to the melted wax—try pine needles, lavender, rosemary, or orange peel.

TINDER

Tinder is the foundation of a fire. If you don't have firelighters, or prefer to practice fire building in its purest form, tinder is the material that will provide the first fuel for your fire and ignite any kindling. In survival situations, tinder needs to be combustible enough to catch with just the smallest of sparks, but for everyday fires, as long as it's dry and easily lit with a match, you're in business.

There are quite a number of household and natural plant materials that work as tinder, and they always have three things in common—they have to be very dry, light, and airy (if something is fluffy, it has a large surface area, which makes it easier to ignite).

In the home, tinder needs to be sustainable and cost-efficient, so scrunched-up newspaper is usually the first choice (avoid glossy magazines and gift wrap; they don't burn well and can release noxious fumes). Wood shavings, cardboard toilet paper rolls, brown paper bags, strands of dry plant material, and pinecones also make excellent starter fuel. If you want to add a fragrant note to the fire, dried orange peel makes a pleasing and crackly fire starter; birch bark and dried rosemary will also work well.

In a survival situation, or if you have no other means of lighting an indoor fire, you can resort to lint (from your pocket or the lint catcher in your dryer), steel wool, potato chips, candle stubs, cigarette filters, dry moss, tampons, cotton balls, string, dry grasses / pine needles / leaves, and plants with fluffy seed heads (such as milkweed, bulrushes, catkins, and dandelions).

KINDLING

Once you've got your tinder or firelighters lit, it's the kindling's turn to do its work. It needs to burn long enough to set fire to the first few logs, so make sure it's dry, thinly split, and stacked with plenty of air space in between.

Some things make better kindling than others. Softwood comes into its own here—the sap-rich timber makes it ideal for easy lighting and fast burning—and if you can get hold of "fatwood," the resin-impregnated heartwood of coniferous trees, even better. Cedar wood also makes good kindling.

If you are splitting your own kindling, aim for as small as you dare—invariably, you'll get a mix of sizes, but if you're averaging sticks of about ¾ inch by ¾ inch (2 centimeters by 2 centimeters), that's perfect. Make as much kindling in one go as you can, and don't scrimp on it when you're laying the fire—it can take a surprising amount of heat to ignite the first thick logs. Keep a generous metal bucketful near the fire; the rest can be stored outside, bagged up or kept in bins until it's needed.

You can also supplement your kindling with other shreds of natural material. Dry bark, birch or sycamore twigs, lumber scraps, dry corncobs, and large pinecones will all help your fire burn.

MATCHES AND LIGHTERS

Does it really matter what you light your fire with? Probably not. But in terms of convenience and chances of not getting singed, some products are better than others.

EXTRA-LONG MATCHES—A normal, short match gives you about six seconds before it reaches your fingers. For most fireplaces and campfires, this just isn't enough time to light the tinder or newspaper, especially if you want it to catch in more than one place. Extra-long matches are perfect for two reasons—not only do they give you more time to light the fire, often three or four times longer, but they also allow you to place the flame right inside the heart of your kindling and tinder. They're also called hearth matches or long-reach matches.

BARBECUE GAS LIGHTERS—If you've got children and don't want matches hanging around, long-necked gas lighters are a good alternative. They also allow a long reach into the fire and will keep a flame alive for more than enough time to get things started. Look for lighters that have child-safety locks and are refillable.

WATERPROOF MATCHES—Sometimes called stormproof matches, these ingenious igniters have an extra-large head and will light (and stay lit) even in heavy wind or rain. They don't give you a long burn—usually only about ten seconds—so you wouldn't want them for everyday hearth use, but they are an absolute lifesaver on a camping trip or survival expedition.

HOW TO STRIKE A MATCH

How to strike a match may seem obvious, but if you're down to your last few matches and they keep snapping or going out, it's important to know you're doing it right.

1. Kneel next to the fire. You don't want the match to have to travel any distance to the tinder.
2. Hold the match between your thumb and index finger.
3. Support the head of the match with your middle finger—this reduces the chance of the head snapping off.
4. Turn your hand so your palm is facing downward.
5. Push the match forward along the strike plate—that is, away from you, not toward you. This is for two reasons: one, if the lit head

snaps off you have a fighting chance of it landing on the kindling, and two, it prevents sparks being directed toward your clothing.

And if you're lighting a campfire, you need to think about how the weather will affect the match:

1. **PROTECT THE FLAME.** Use your hands and body to shield the lit match from any gusts or driving rain.
2. **LIGHT THE BASE OF THE FIRE.** The first precious flames will travel upward through the fuel and have less chance of being blown out or extinguished by rain.
3. **FACE DOWNWIND.** You want the wind to be behind you. This does two things: your body is shielding the campfire from any driving weather, and you're reducing the chance of flames leaping back in your direction.

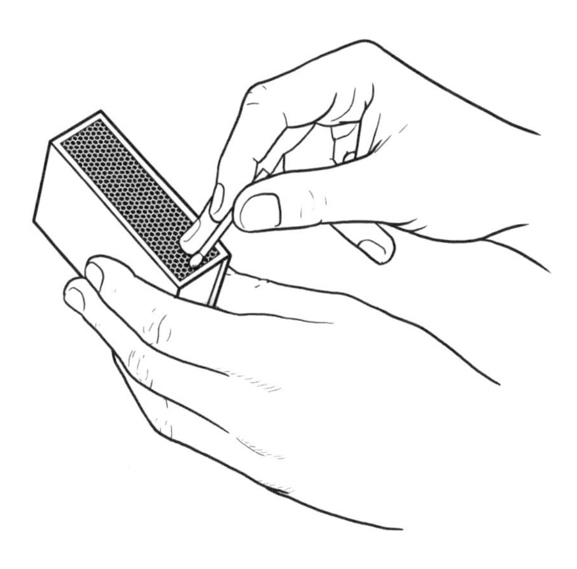

HOW TO USE NEWSPAPER

Talk to ten different fire enthusiasts and you'll get ten different newspaper techniques. Some prefer the rolled newspaper technique, others shred, but most people stick to scrunching up newspaper into tight balls.

If you look at the science, there's actually sound logic behind the scrunching technique. When you scrunch up a large piece of paper into spheres, it does three things, all of which help you if you are lighting a fire:

1. Scrunching paper increases the surface area of the paper relative to the size of the ball. A grapefruit-size ball of newspaper is relatively small, but thanks to its many folds and creases, it has a huge surface area. Put a handful of these paper balls into a fireplace, and you have crammed a generous amount of potential fuel into a fairly restricted space.
2. Scrunched-up paper is incredibly strong and can bear a substantial weight on top of it, which is perfect for stacking kindling and logs on top. Try doing the same with shredded newspaper; it just doesn't work.

3. Even when you scrunch newspaper into the smallest ball you can manage, it's still 90 percent air. Air plus fuel equals the perfect recipe for combustion.

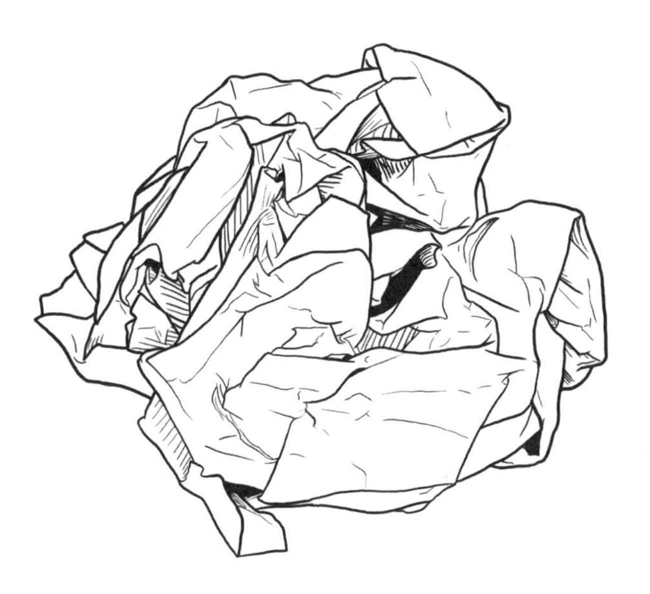

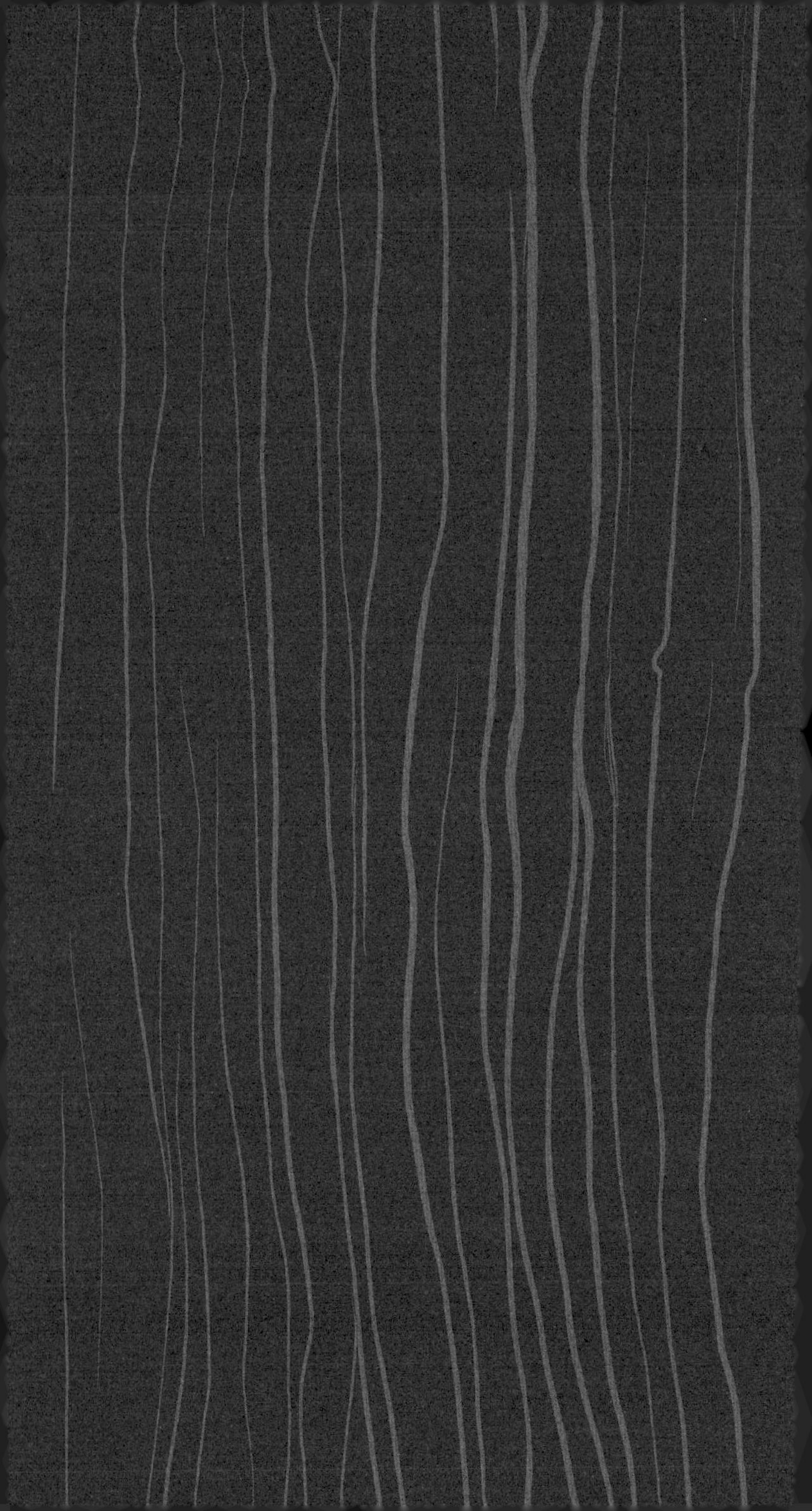

CHAPTER SIX

Building a Fire

He sat in the snow, pulling the sticks from the bushes under the trees and feeding them directly to the flame. He knew he must not fail. When it is 75 below zero, a man must not fail in his first attempt to build a fire.

—JACK LONDON, "TO BUILD A FIRE"

WHICH FIRE TO BUILD?

Now we're getting to the fun part. There are dozens of different ways to construct a fire, each with an army of faithful supporters. Until recently, most people relied on the traditional bottom-up fire, with newspaper and kindling at the base and logs on the top. In recent years, fire enthusiasts have been extolling the virtues of the top-down fire, the counter-intuitive method of upside-down burning (see The Top-Down Fire, page 108).

The reality is that every fire, fireplace, and wood-stove is different. Timber supplies vary, as do airflow and access to good kindling. This makes it difficult to generalize; what works for one home may not for another. The trick is to experiment. Work out which method suits the size and idiosyncrasies of your hearth or woodstove.

If you're outdoors, the weather conditions may influence what kind of fire you build—the lean-to fire, for example, is a good one to build if you need to protect the fledgling flames from wind or driving rain. If you want to cook on your fire with some degree of control, the cowboy fire is an excellent option.

Whichever method you choose, if you are outdoors you can also boost any heat the fire kicks out by building a simple reflector. Push two thin poles into the ground, leaning slightly away from the fire. Stack logs horizontally up the sticks to create a barrier, or lean anything reflective against them, and this will throw back some of that lost heat.

THE BOTTOM-UP FIRE

Whether you build a tepee of sticks or the more complex log cabin, this type of fire essentially burns from the bottom up. The logic of this is that flames flicker upward and ignite the fuel above. In practice, radiant heat travels in multiple directions (which is why the top-down fire also works), but this method has the advantage of keeping your newspaper or tinder dry if there's any rain. You can also build a smaller, quicker fire this way, keeping it to just a few sticks. With all bottom-up fires, leave putting the largest logs on until you are confident the fire has taken hold.

THE TEPEE

Start with the tinder or firelighter in the middle, and lean the kindling sticks over it, tips pointing upward, to create a wigwam shape. If the stack is stable enough, you can build up the sides with progressively larger logs.

SUITABLE FOR: *Open fires, woodstoves, and campfires. Simple, easy, and doesn't need much initial fuel—perfect for a small fire.*

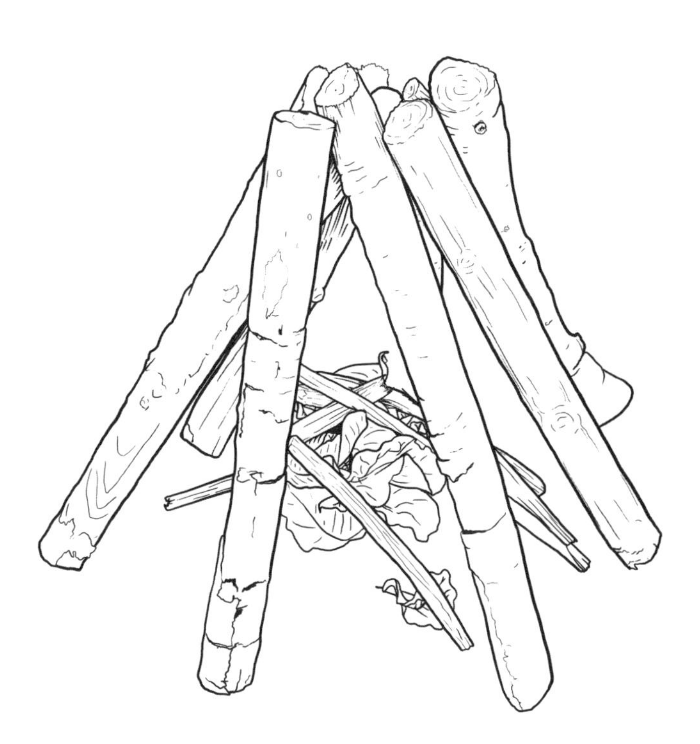

THE LOG CABIN

Take two kindling sticks and place them parallel to each other, about 4 inches (10 centimeters) apart. Take two more sticks and balance them across the first two, creating four sides of a square. Continue stacking pairs of kindling until you are about six layers high. Fill the middle with tinder and then make a "roof" from a layer of kindling topped with thin logs.

SUITABLE FOR: *Open fires and campfires. A bit too fussy for a woodstove. This arrangement takes longer to build but is low maintenance and slow burning once lit.*

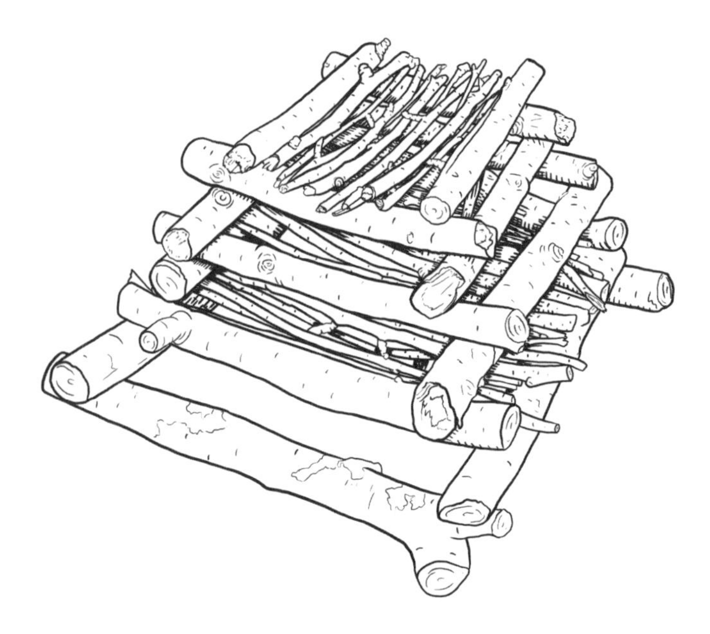

THE SANDWICH

This is a traditional hearth fire. Start with a layer of crumpled newspaper or firelighters. Add three layers of kindling (crisscross the layers and leave plenty of air gaps), followed by two or three narrow logs.

SUITABLE FOR: *Open fires and woodstoves, but not ideal for campfires as it struggles to catch if windy. This arrangement is quick to build and lights relatively easily.*

THE TOP-DOWN FIRE

If you haven't tried this method, do. Even if it's just to prove that it works. It feels completely counterintuitive, after years of building fires from the bottom up, but more often than not it produces results. It's also a handy technique for woodstoves, which often have a log guard or grill at the front that can make accessing the base of a fire tricky.

Top-down fires don't perform as well if the logs or tinder aren't dry enough, if there isn't enough room in the woodstove to create a decent stack, or if you're outdoors and there's a chance your tinder will be blown away or rained on before it's had a chance to catch. It's also a fire stack that needs a generous amount of kindling to work, so if you're in short supply, stick to the tepee (see The Tepee, page 105).

Indoors, the top-down method has the advantage of pre-warming the flue, which helps draw the smoke up the chimney, and it also allows you to make a relatively large fire in one go, letting you get on with other things. The trick with this fire is to take your time while you are building it—the more stable the structure, the less likely it is to collapse and potentially go out.

1. Lay your largest logs in a row on the hearth, ground, or in the base of your woodstove. Leave a 1-inch (2.5-centimeter) gap between them to allow for air movement.
2. Take your narrow logs and lay them on top, perpendicular to the first row.
3. Continue with two or three layers of kindling, again perpendicular to each other, and top with a final layer of tinder or newspaper. Secure the tinder or paper with a few extra sticks of kindling on top.

SUITABLE FOR: *Large open fires, woodstoves, and campfires (only in good weather). Takes some time to build and uses lots of kindling, but has the advantage of pre-warming the flue, helping it draw.*

THE LEAN-TO FIRE

The lean-to fire is a good option if you are out in the sticks and struggling against the elements, as the inherent design of the fire acts as a windbreak to protect the first flames. It's also a very stable structure.

1. Find a thick, dry log and use this as your "brace log." You could also use a large stone.
2. Lean small twigs or any other kindling against the brace log, making sure they are on the downwind side (i.e., the brace log is shielding the twigs from the wind). You can make this fire as short or as tall as you wish, depending on how far along the log you prop your kindling.
3. Fill underneath the kindling with dry tinder.
4. Once the fire is established, keep adding fuel to the downwind side of the log, but don't prop it against the brace log. The brace log will char and burn very slowly, acting more as a windbreak than the focus of the fire. In fact, once the embers are glowing, you can add another brace log on the other side of the fire, parallel to the first, and you have yourself a makeshift cooking platform.

SUITABLE FOR: *Campfires, even if the weather's bad. Can be turned into a cooking fire. Will work as an indoor fire, but the brace log can take up too much space in a small hearth or woodstove.*

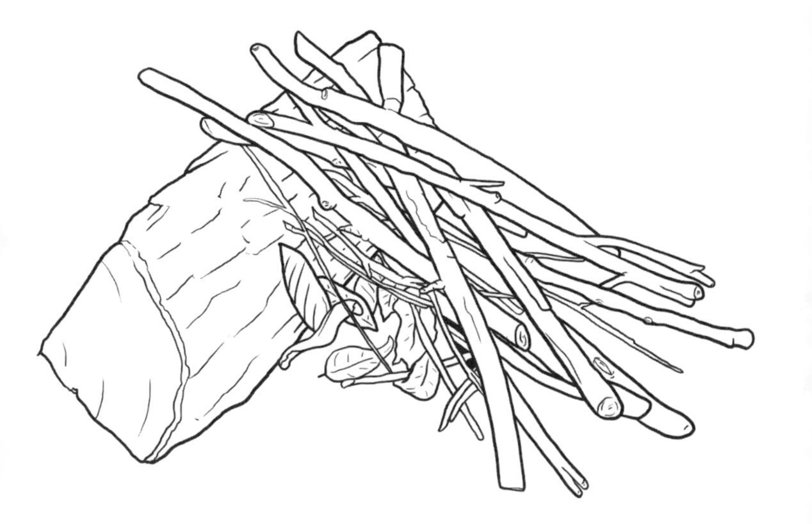

THE COWBOY FIRE

This name conjures up images of Wild West cowboys eating beans out of mess tins. In reality, this fire, also called the star fire, isn't particularly practical to sit around because the radiating "spokes" of the fire are a bit of a trip hazard and keep you at a distance from the heat.

What it does make is an excellent cooking fire. This is because all the heat is focused into one small, intense spot—ideal for straddling with a metal tripod and hanging a cooking pot. Because the ends of the logs are also near each other, they make the perfect platform for resting a metal grill or griddle pan on.

It's also perfect for outdoors if you have no means of cutting long lengths of timber down; as the fire nibbles away the ends of the logs, you simply push them farther into the center.

1. Lay between six and ten long logs in a star shape (like the spokes of a wheel).
2. Where the spokes meet in the middle, leave a gap the size of a salad plate and fill with tinder. On top of this, layer plenty of kindling. The kindling should be long enough to stretch across the gap and sit on the ends of the logs. This helps with airflow.

3. Keep adding tinder and small pieces of fuel until the ends of the logs start to burn. Once the fire is well established, remember to keep nudging the logs into the heat.

SUITABLE FOR: *Campfires and large open fires. Too big for a woodstove—the large footprint needs a generous hearth space. Great for cooking, uses little wood, and slow burning.*

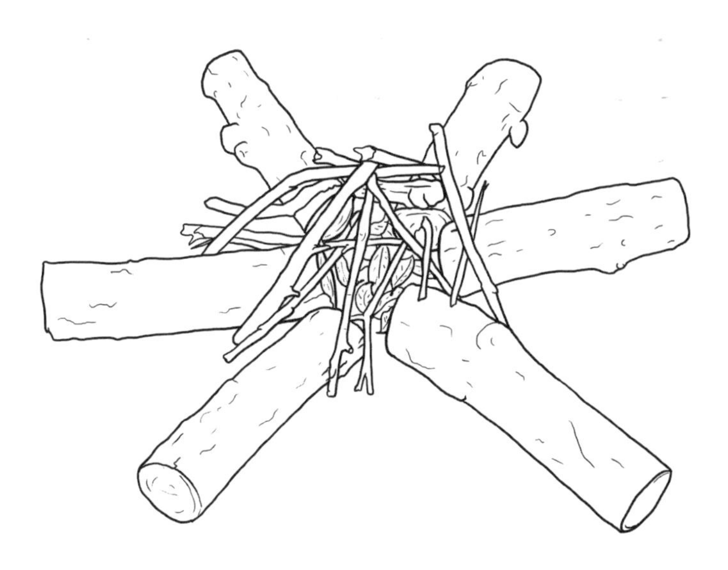

FIRESIDE TOOLS

Every indoor fireside needs a set of tools. These aren't just quaint decorative items, but tools you'll use every time you build, burn, and clean up after a fire. Here's what the set should contain:

POKER—This is best used for maneuvering burning materials around the fireplace and, when the fire is over, spreading out the hot embers. Coal benefits from regular prodding, but don't be tempted to overdo it with a wood fire; all you'll get is a shower of sparks. Get a poker with a hook so you can pull logs as well as push them.

TONGS—Should the occasional piece of burning material escape or get out of place, tongs are essential. Don't get coal tongs, which are essentially like a large pair of tweezers; you need log tongs, which have a scissor action that can grab large pieces of wood.

BRUSH AND METAL SHOVEL—These tools are needed for ash removal and removing debris brought in with the log basket. The brush needs to have robust natural bristles (e.g., coir) that won't melt on contact with heat.

HEATPROOF GLOVES—These are handy if you have a woodstove with a metal door handle or air vent that gets hot during operation. They can also double as protection from splintery logs and kindling.

BELLOWS—These give a struggling fire the extra boost of air it needs to take hold. To use bellows, aim the nozzle at pieces of glowing timber, and blow only until they start to flame. On a new fire, go gently; you don't want to blow out the first flames.

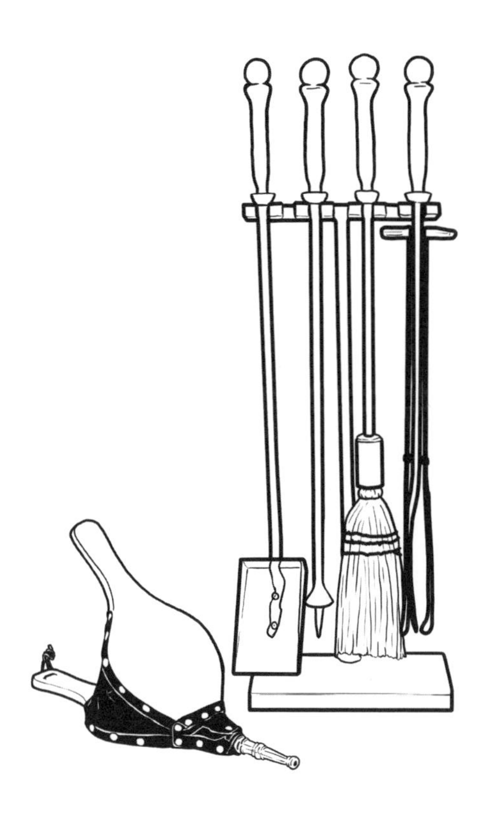

STAYING SAFE INDOORS

Unfortunately, most fire-related accidents happen indoors. Anyone who uses a fire, or lives in a home heated by wood, should be aware of these potential hazards so you can take steps to prevent accidents and keep everyone safe:

- Keep flues clean and well maintained—this reduces the chance of a chimney fire.
- Have your chimney swept at least twice a year if you are burning logs—at the beginning and in the middle of the season.
- Make sure there is plenty of ventilation.
- Always get woodstoves and flues fitted by a qualified professional.
- Use a strong mesh guard to protect against flying sparks.
- Keep children away from open fires and woodstoves—use a safety guard with fixed wall brackets.
- Don't go to bed until you are sure that the fire is under control and guarded or, ideally, completely out.
- Don't prop logs against woodstoves, where they can heat up and smolder.
- Don't dry clothes over or near the fire.

- Keep matches, lighters, and firelighters out of reach of children and pets.
- Don't burn wet wood, plastics, trash, or any other materials likely to give off smoke, noxious fumes, or particulates.
- Install smoke and carbon monoxide detectors if you haven't already.

STAYING SAFE OUTDOORS

It's easy to become relaxed and complacent around a roaring campfire, but remember there's a huge responsibility attached to building a fire outdoors. Forest fires are a common occurrence in many parts of the world, and are all too often started by an unwitting camper.

- Always check the weather forecast first. Sudden gusts of wind or changes in wind direction can quickly turn a campfire into a wildfire.
- Choose a safe spot to build your fire. Build on level ground covered with gravel or soil if possible, and steer well clear of overhanging branches, tents, vehicles, fences, and dry grass. Stay at least 10 feet (3 meters) from anything that could catch fire.

- Don't use accelerants to light or revive a fire and, after lighting it, don't throw the match away until you've doused it with water.
- Keep your supply of dry firewood upwind, away from any flying sparks and hot ashes.
- Kids need to be supervised at all times. Teach them how to stop, drop, and roll if their clothing catches fire.
- Never leave your campfire unattended, and keep a bucket of water handy at all times.
- When it's time to go, extinguish the fire by drowning it with water and stirring the embers to make sure everything is cold. Don't bury the embers with soil; they can smolder.

ASHES

This fine, soft, light gray powder is manna from heaven for gardeners because it's full of lime, potassium, and other trace elements that plants need to flourish. Traditionally, wood ash was also used as an abrasive cleaning agent and as an ingredient in soap making, and it still has plenty of uses today:

FERTILIZER—Sprinkle lightly over the beds and lawn or rake into soil. You can also add it to your compost heap, where it'll mellow and add to the richness of the organic matter.

SOIL IMPROVER—Add to very acidic soil (5.5 pH or less) to raise the pH level; tomatoes and other nightshade vegetables love it. Don't use on raspberries, however, which like slightly acidic soil, as do roses and rhododendrons.

PEST REPELLENT—Wood ash makes life very uncomfortable for snails and slugs; place a ring around the most affected plants. Ash has also been known to be effective against aphids when dusted onto tomato plants and eggplants.

HOUSEHOLD CLEANER—Mix with a little water to form a smooth paste, apply it to silverware, and then let it sit for a few minutes. Wipe off and buff to a shine.

DE-ICER—Wood ash also makes a good eco-friendly de-icer, perfect for throwing over pavements and driveways. The ash works mainly by increasing traction, but the salts in ash also have a gentle de-icing effect.

NOTE: *Ashes can stay hot for a long time after the fire has died out. Always store them away from combustible material, in a metal container or bucket.*

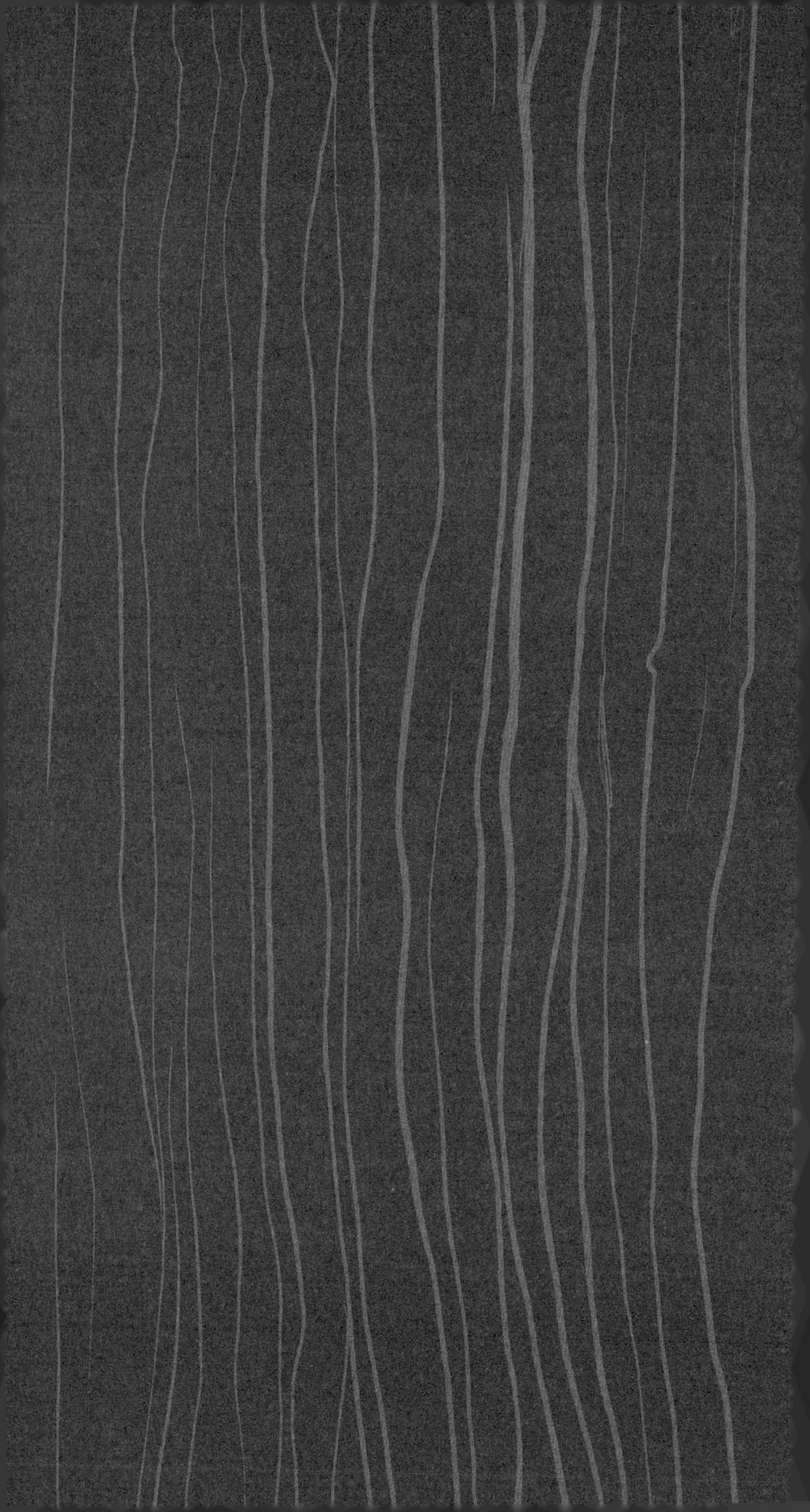

CHAPTER SEVEN

Fragrant Fire

**Old wood best to burn,
old wine to drink,
old friends to trust,
and old authors to read.**

—ALFONSO X OF CASTILE

SCENTED SMOKE

In most instances, you don't want a smoky fire. If your hearth is billowing out gray swirling clouds, you're either burning wet wood, there's not enough oxygen getting to the wood, or your chimney is blocked. But there are a few occasions where smoke is useful, even desirable. If you want to smoke meat or cheese, keep flying insects at bay, or add a whiff of woody scent to a room, a little smoke can go a long way.

There are different ways to get your fire to produce smoke, as you'll see in the following pages, but you are, in essence, deliberately creating a situation where the fire can't combust completely. When wood fuel can't combust completely, not everything is burned away, and what you can see are tiny unburned particles of things like tar, carbon (soot), oils, and ash floating upward with the fire's warm convected air.

Of course you'll need to be careful about inhaling soot, as there's no doubt that persistent exposure to lungfuls of sooty smoke is not only irritating but also potentially harmful in the long term. But that isn't what we're aiming for—we're talking about scented smoke wafting through the air to draw you close to the fire, spices and herbs crackling in the open flames, and gently smoldering applewood chips. Think of the fragrant fire as a huge incense stick—an ancient device to give out warming, aromatic wisps of delicious smoke. In fact, the word *perfume* comes from the Latin *perfumare*, meaning "to smoke through," from a time when smoke was used not only for room fragrance but also for religious rituals and purification.

PERFUMED WOOD

Not all wood smells delicious when it burns, but there's an array of species that will add wisps of pleasant, aromatic smoke to an open fire. Most of the smoke will appear at the beginning of your evening, when the fire isn't hot enough to combust completely, so make the most of this time to add your fragrant kindling and logs. Once the fire is well established, you can, if you're careful, use a poker to separate a log from the others and allow it to smolder gently without flames for a few minutes before pushing it back into the heart of the fire.

Picking which scents you like comes down to personal preference—one person's perfume is another's pollutant—but most people find that fruit trees such as apple, cherry, pear, fig, and plum give off a gentle, subtly sweet scent. Soft coniferous woods, such as pine and spruce, produce a pleasant, resinous smoke, while nut species like hazel and walnut add oaty, autumnal notes.

Some of the hardwoods—oak, elm, ash, and birch—have homey, campfire smells, but the stars of the show have to be cedar, hickory, and mesquite, three woods that you don't often see sold as firewood but have the most fantastically evocative smoke (and are sold as chips—see Smoking Food, page 135). Other richly scented woods that don't often get logged but may come your way in the form of garden cuttings and branches include eucalyptus, olive, bay, and cypress.

PINECONES

There are few things more wintery than the smell of spruce. Pinecones—those woody, tactile pockets of scent—are the perfect way to capture that feeling, and make excellent kindling for an aromatic fire.

Despite their seasonal connotations, pinecones actually drop throughout most of the year, depending on the species of tree, weather conditions, and whether the cone is male or female. Autumn is probably the most fruitful time to go a-hunting, so gather and keep as many basketfuls as you dare, to dry out and store by the fire.

The pinecone makes a particularly good fire starter for two reasons: first, those thin wood scales are perfect for catching sunlight and help the cone dry out to a useful moisture level, and second, their glorious sticky resin is highly flammable. As with all pine material, burning pinecones can leave a small amount of creosote deposit on the inside of the chimney, but with the volumes you'll burn the impact will be minimal and negated by a twice-yearly sweep.

For maximum combustion, make sure the pinecones are lovely and dry, with the prickles as open as possible. Some people actually dry theirs in a low oven first—a thirty-minute blast is ample—and then add a few drops of pine essential oil to each cone for extra fragrance. Use a handful at a time.

HERB BUNDLES

The idea of herb bundles (also called smudge sticks and herb cakes) isn't a new one. For thousands of years, people have used aromatic smoke to bless, cleanse, and heal—ceremonies and sacred spaces were filled with the scents of burning herbs, resin, and bark. In medieval times, herbs were dried and tied ready to toss onto an open fire to sweeten the air and stave off ill health.

The best time to make herb bundles is after the summer growth has died down, when you're pruning back those woody aromatic herbs. Start well before the first frosts—not only will this give the plants time to recover, but you'll also have created a nice dry basketful of herb bundles ready for the log-fire season.

You need cuttings or prunings of about 6 inches (15 centimeters). Choose any fragrant herbs—the woodier the better, as they'll survive the drying process intact. Rosemary, bay, lavender, eucalyptus, thyme, lemon verbena, sage—there's a whole apothecary of herbs to try. Tie a handful together with natural string or raffia, and experiment with combinations of herbs for different aromas.

These fragrant bundles will not only gently perfume the living room while stacked patiently in a basket, but throw a few on the fire, either at the very beginning or on the embers at the very end, and you'll also be rewarded with a gentle waft of incense-like smoke.

PEEL AND SPICES

Citrus peel and spices add a heady, mulled-wine note to the fragrant fire. Because the components are smaller and fussier, you need to wrap them in newspaper; making candy wrapper–like twists works quite well, and the shape makes them easier to light at one end.

Whole spices are expensive, so this is a good way to recycle aromatics that have already had one round in a recipe. Vanilla pods scraped of their seeds still have lots of sweet-smelling potential, as do cinnamon pods that have been simmered, cloves from a ham, or bay leaves fished out of a stockpot. Just dry them off and add to the mix.

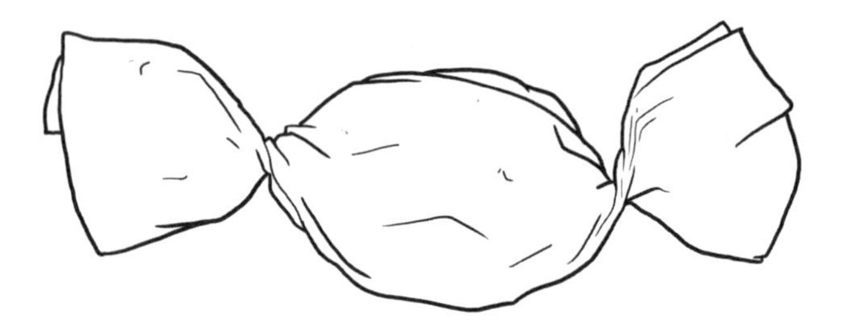

Similarly, store-bought citrus peel is too expensive to burn, but you can easily dry your own anywhere that's warm and airy. Lay on a plate and rest it on the stove top or propped on a radiator, and the peel will be dry in days. Tangerine, satsuma, orange, lemon, and clementine peels are wonderful oily fire starters and really give these bundles some oomph.

TO MAKE THE BUNDLES:

1. Take a large sheet of newspaper and fold along the crease. Use black-and-white pages only (colored ink or glossy pages can release noxious fumes).
2. At one end of the sheet, place a handful of dried citrus peel and whole spices—cloves, cinnamon sticks, star anise, cardamom pods, cumin seeds, coriander seeds, used vanilla pods, spent coffee grounds, fennel seeds. Create your own blend, but always include plenty of peel, as that's the tinder that will really catch.
3. Roll up the newspaper and twist both ends to make a candy wrapper shape—this will keep the spices from falling out. Use in place of other tinder.

FRAGRANT FIRELIGHTERS

Traditional firelighters do the job but contribute very little to the fragrant fire. At best, they're odorless; at worst, they can leave a pungent whiff of burning fossil fuels and give an unpleasant tinge to food if you're cooking on an outdoor fire.

If you want the convenience but don't want to sacrifice scent, there are an increasing number of natural firelighters on the market, ready to light, and studded with delicious-smelling herbs, spices, and peel. Some are wax-based, usually soy or beeswax, as that gives a less polluting burn. They are often perfumed with essential oils—orange or cinnamon, for example—and then topped with woody notes such as cinnamon shavings and star anise.

Pinecones set into wax are another eco-option (see Homemade Firelighters, page 90 for a DIY version). The wax is a good vehicle for other flammable ingredients, such as pine needles and wood shavings. You can even set them into old cardboard egg cartons, so can you just tear off a segment and throw it into the fire.

A less well-known option is ocote firesticks. Ocote is a fast-growing timber from Central America traditionally used by the Mayan people for lighting fires. The species is a member of the coniferous family and has a naturally high resin content that catches fire quickly, making it ideal fodder for fire lighting. Ocote also has the good fortune of being highly fragrant, and once lit, produces an intense and deliciously piney perfume—perfect for fans of scented smoke.

ESSENTIAL OILS

It's worth prefacing anything about perfumes and fragrant fires with the gentle warning that essential oils are highly flammable, so it's not ideal to start throwing them onto hot embers or naked flames. Don't even keep the bottle near the fire.

But their very flammability, combined with their potent fragrance, makes them eminently useful when added as an ingredient to wax firelighters, or if a few drops of heady scent are left to soak into and dry onto pinecones or other tinder and kindling. This has the added benefit of turning your pinecone basket into a huge potpourri, exuding welcoming scents even when the fire is out.

Certain scents work better than others. The smell of burning rose oil, the epitome of a summer's day, for example, can feel incongruous on a cozy winter's evening, so choose essential oils that capture those resinous, evocative aromas of log piles and herb bundles (see Herb Bundles, page 128), or conjure up wintery celebrations and memories:

SANDALWOOD—sweet, warm, rich, masculine, and woody

CYPRESS—clean, fresh, herbaceous, slightly evergreen

CEDARWOOD—soft, woody, not unlike pencil shavings

FRANKINCENSE—sweetly spicy, honeyed, slightly fruity

MYRHH—smoky, sweet, earthy, some say licorice-like

PINE—fresh, foresty, like Christmas in a bottle

CINNAMON—warm, homey, spicy, the smell of baking

EUCALYPTUS—strong, camphor-like, reminiscent of vapor rub

SMOKING FOOD

Fragrant smoke triggers all kinds of primal responses. Just as we feel comforted and protected by the smell of an open fire, so too are our taste buds sharpened by a whiff of woody smoke. As humans, we associate the smell of fire not only with heat and security, but also with the anticipation of cooked food—our inner caveman doesn't lie far below the surface.

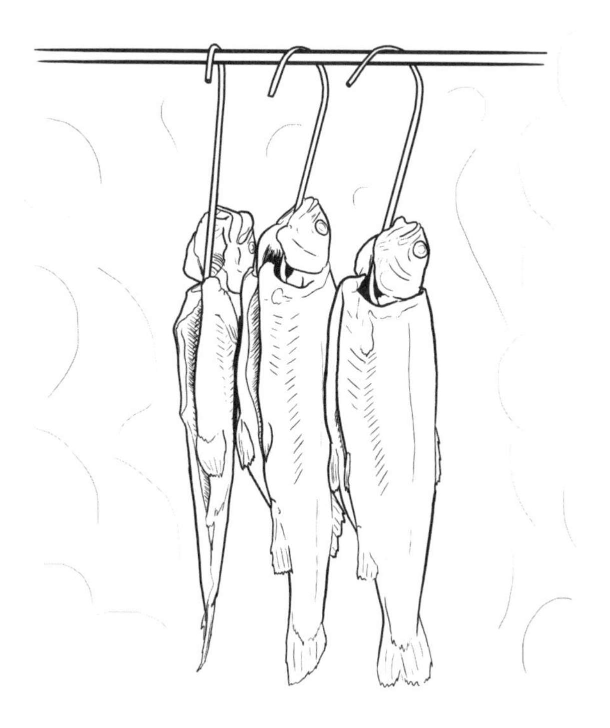

The process is subtle, and you can tweak the results depending on the type of woodchips or shavings you burn. Woodsmoke varies in flavor from mild to strong; delicate foods that you don't want to overpower—salmon, vegetables, cheeses, and chicken—need a light touch, while gutsier meats—beef, lamb, game, and pork—are transformed with strongly flavored woods:

APPLE—a gentle, fruity smoke flavor that works with poultry, fish, and pork. All the fruit woods are mild flavored and ideal for smoking cheeses, butter, and vegetables.

OAK—a mellow, well-rounded smoky flavor, delicious with almost every foodstuff. You can also buy oak chips from whiskey barrels, which gives an extra dimension to the flavor.

MAPLE—another mellow-flavored smoke that adds a sweet, subtle taste perfect for poultry, game birds, ham, and cheeses.

HICKORY—the quintessential flavor of smoked bacon. Strongly flavored, so works best with pork, ribs, and other barbecue favorites.

MESQUITE—very strongly flavored, but slightly sweeter than hickory, and pairs best with rich, red meats, such as steak, duck, and lamb.

SMOKE AND ALLERGIES

Not everyone finds smoke pleasant. While most of us thrill at the sight of a roaring fire, there are some people who find smoke difficult to tolerate, particularly those with any kind of respiratory problem.

Fireplaces, for all their contemplative coziness, throw far more smoke and irritating particles back into the room than a closed woodstove does, so if you suffer from allergies or asthma, you may find that investing in a certified woodstove helps.

Air pollution is also worse if wood isn't seasoned properly, the chimney is clogged, or there isn't adequate airflow getting to the fuel. Keeping to sensible wood fuel practices, such as never burning wet wood, getting your chimney swept twice a year, and making sure you know how to work the air vents on your woodstove, is essential.

Some people find the mold on firewood can trigger problems, so if that's the case, don't store your logs indoors and only bring them in when you are ready to burn them. Other irritants might come from other things that are being burned, such as petrochemical firelighters, trash, plastics, or colored paper. All these steps may help, but if you still find your symptoms are worsened by woodsmoke, you may need to reduce or eliminate your exposure altogether.

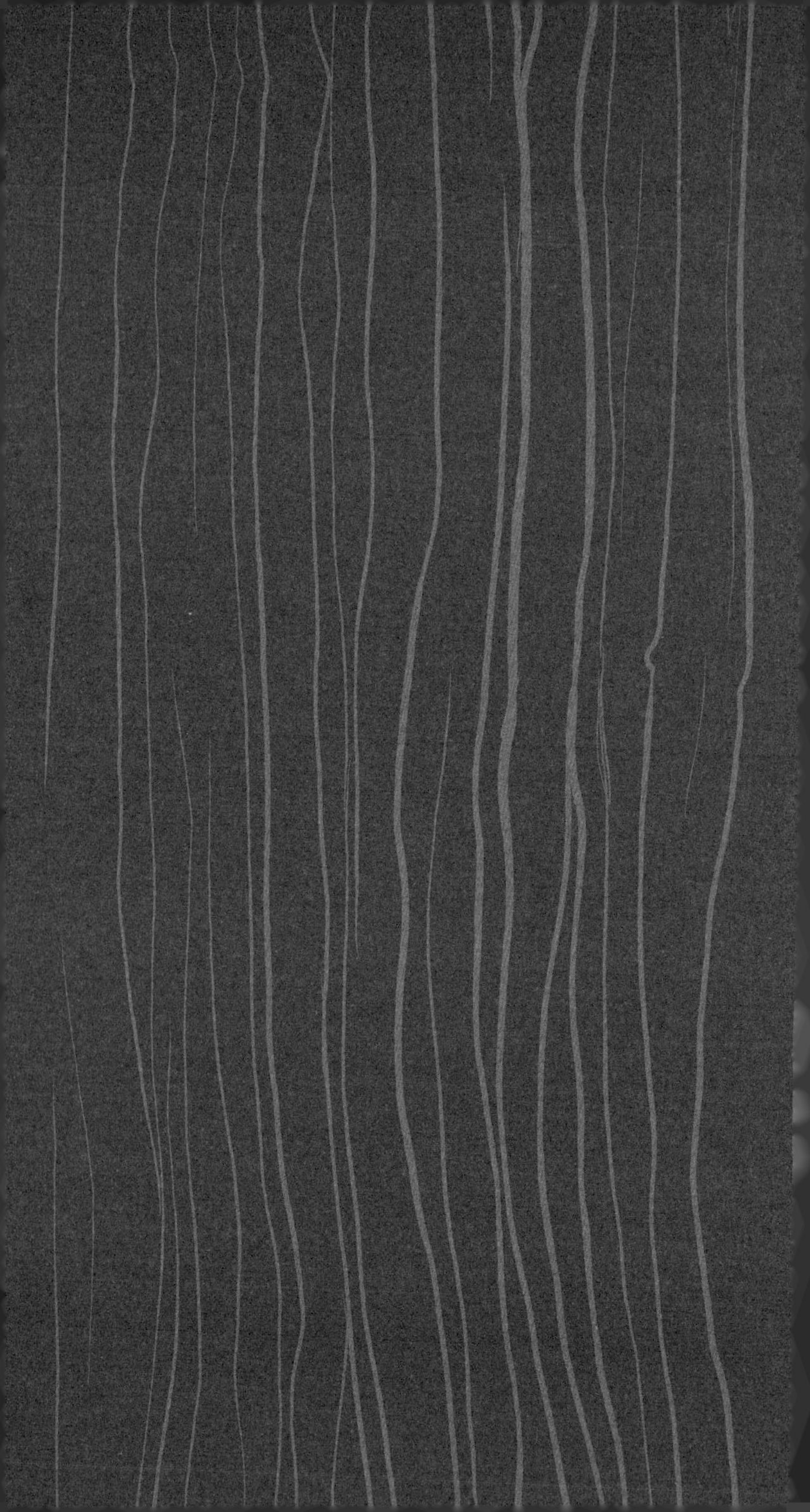

CHAPTER EIGHT

Fire Safety

Man is the only creature that dares to light a fire and live with it. The reason? Because he alone has learned to put it out.

—HENRY JACKSON VAN DYKE JR., *FISHERMAN'S LUCK AND SOME OTHER UNCERTAIN THINGS*

THE YEARLY CHECKUP

Your fireplace or woodstove is a tool, to be looked after, cleaned, and repaired if necessary—do this and it will give you a long life of efficient, companionable warmth in return. When domestic fires go wrong, nine times out of ten it comes down to poor maintenance, so here's a list of things you should check at least once a year, preferably well before the burning season gets going. Most people get their flues swept and buy fuel when the nights turn cool, but if you plan ahead you'll beat the rush and may even find things cheaper than during peak season.

GET YOUR FUEL SUPPLY—Don't misjudge and have to wait for logs to arrive. Buy early and get some extra seasoning time under your belt.

CALL THE SWEEP—Get the detritus from last winter's burn out of your flue before you spark up for the new season. If you are burning lots of wood, you may need an extra sweep midseason.

SERVICE THE WOODSTOVE—Check the condition of the key parts of your woodstove, such as the baffle plate, the rope seal around the door, and the firebricks at the back.

CLEAN THE GLASS—Even with good-quality fuel and a healthy airflow, your stove's door will have a tendency to blacken, especially at the corners. Use stove glass cleaner, and always wait until the woodstove is cool before you start.

SWEEPS

Having your chimney swept is an absolute necessity. A chimney must be clear to allow noxious gases to pass up and out of your home instead of billowing back into your living room. Regular sweeping also removes all the sooty deposits that build up on the lining of the flue or brickwork, helping to prevent dangerous chimney fires.

While you can help reduce the likelihood of a blocked chimney by doing all the sensible things like not burning wet wood or banking up for overnight burning, the only surefire way to keep safe is to get it professionally swept. A qualified sweep will brush away the deposits from last season's fires, check that the flue isn't blocked with nests or debris, and keep an eye on the condition of key parts of your woodstove or fireplace. Some insurance companies now insist on regular sweeping and will ask for paperwork to prove it.

If you want to find a reputable sweep, the best place to start is a regulatory trade organization (see Resources, page 156). To be a member of any of these bodies, candidates have to undergo training, be fully insured, and work to a code of practice. And if you've never had your chimney swept before, don't be put off by visions of soot-covered brooms and clouds of dust—modern sweeps use strong vacuums, floor coverings, and specialized tools to create minimal disruption and mess.

FIRE AND FURNITURE

A blazing fire is the beating heart of any room, the focal point around which everyone and everything should converge. It gives structure to a living space, a kinetic centerpiece that holds our attention and gives a room character and ambience. It's always good to position your furniture to capitalize on this coziness, but make sure you're being safe. Here are some tips to keep in mind when arranging your furniture near the fireplace:

- Stick to the 1-yard (1-meter) rule—have nothing that is flammable, whether it's your sofa or your log basket, closer than 3 feet (1 meter) from the fire.
- Don't put mirrors above an open fireplace. People can end up standing too close to the flames and risk their clothes catching fire.

- Anything that is upholstered needs to meet current fire-resistance standards—look for the label.
- Antiques and pre-1950s furniture are exempt from the standards, but it doesn't make them any less flammable. Keep these items farther away from the fire.
- All fabrics can burn, but some are more resistant to catching fire than others. Pure wool, for example, is naturally slow to burn, while polyester-cotton blends can ignite and spread quickly.
- A hearth rug will not only soften the room but also protect a carpet or wooden floor from potential sparks. It must be flame resistant—look for those woven from flameproof fiberglass yarn, or natural fibers such as pure wool, jute, or sisal, all of which are naturally fire retardant.

FIRE SAFETY WITH CHILDREN

Children find fire mesmerizing. The life-enhancing skill of learning to build a fire is an important lesson, but only under the careful supervision of an adult. Fire is one of the most common causes of accidental injury and death among children, so it's vital that you teach them to respect and understand the dangers, and make your hearth and home as safe as possible.

Give clear, unambiguous instructions of dos and don'ts around fire. With young children under five, you will have to keep reinforcing the message. Key things to tell them include:

» Never to play with matches or lighters.
» If they see matches or lighters lying around, to tell a grown-up.
» Not to play or leave toys near an open fire or woodstove.

As a responsible adult, the onus is on you to remove as many dangers as possible. It's all common sense but easy to overlook if you're busy or distracted:

» Don't leave young children on their own in a room where there's an open fire or lit woodstove.
» Keep matches, lighters, and firelighters out of reach or locked away. Only use lighters with child-resistant features.
» Use a childproof fireguard in front of an open fire or woodstove (see Fireguards, page 146).
» Teach kids to stop, drop, and roll—they'll love practicing this, but it's a lifesaver if clothes accidentally catch fire.

» Make sure your children know what the smoke detector sounds like, and practice, as a family, how you would escape and call 911.

FIREGUARDS

There are two basic types of fireguard: the spark guard, which is a fine metal mesh designed to keep hot sparks from going astray, and the child-safety guard, a cage or fence-like guard with the sole purpose of keeping young kids at a safe distance from the source of heat.

Spark guards can be simple flat screens, which are useful if you have a large, recessed hearth and just need to cover the front of the fire. Most fireplaces, however, are safer with a hinged or folding guard, which can catch any stray sparks that ping off at a tangent.

Child-safety guards must create a physical barrier between the fire or hot stove and little fingers. Most manufacturers recommend a clear space of at least 30 inches (75 centimeters) between the guard and the heat source. The guard also needs to be far enough away from direct heat so as not to become dangerously hot to touch. Child guards are designed to be fixed to the wall so a toddler can't fall and push the guard onto the flames or pull it on top of him or herself. These types of guards don't offer any spark protection, however, as the bars or grill meshes are too widely spaced, so if you have a fireplace and kids you'll need both types of guard.

Woodstoves, while spark-safe, still need a child-safety guard—kids (and vulnerable adults) may not realize that even though the flame is safely contained, the metal is searingly hot to touch.

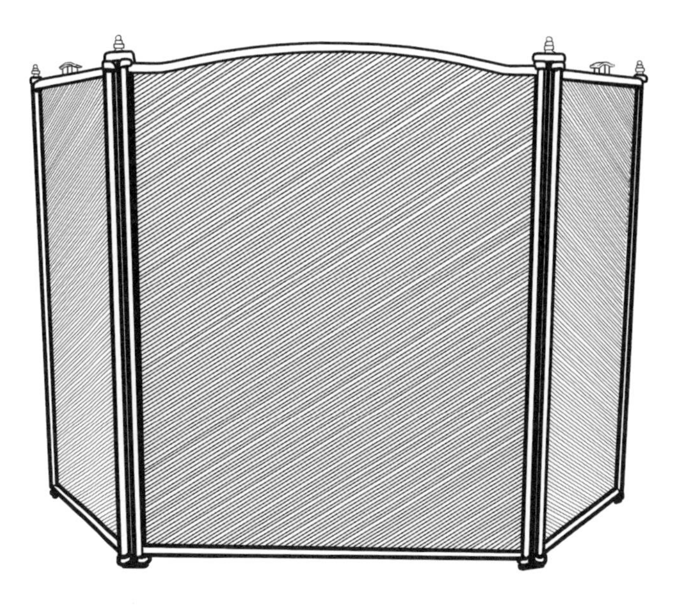

CARBON MONOXIDE AND SMOKE DETECTORS

Carbon monoxide (CO) is produced when fuels such as gas, coal, and wood don't burn fully. Blocked chimneys, badly fitted woodstoves, and inadequate ventilation can all cause dangerous levels of CO to build up, with potentially fatal consequences. You can't smell, taste, or see carbon monoxide, which is what makes it so deadly, but symptoms can include headaches, dizziness, and loss of consciousness.

Along with getting your chimney swept regularly and having any stove installed by a qualified engineer, you *must* install a carbon monoxide detector in any room with a fire. CO alarms are a legal requirement with stoves installed after 2010, and any stove in a rented property.

There are guidelines about where to install your CO detector. If you attach it to the ceiling, the detector must be at least 12 inches (30 centimeters) away from the wall. Alternatively, it can be at head height, either on the wall or a shelf, approximately 3 to 10 feet (1 to 3 meters) away from the fire. Make sure nothing is covering or obstructing the alarm, and don't install it too close to a window, door, or fan, or inside a cupboard or closet. Test the alarm once a week by pressing the "test" or "reset" button.

Along with a CO detector, every home needs a smoke detector, especially if you are using a fire-place. Most fire services recommend at least one detector on every floor, but ideally one detector in every room you use regularly. Again, these need testing once a week. Many companies sell carbon monoxide and smoke detectors in one unit.

HOW TO CHECK A WOODSTOVE

Woodstoves are brilliantly simple, robust devices. There's not much that can go wrong with them, and when parts do wear out, they're relatively easy to fix. That said, if you've never owned one before, problems aren't always obvious without knowing what to look for. If you've inherited one with a house move, you must get the chimney swept and the stove looked over before you use it (see Sweeps, page 142). The rest of the time, here are a few things to check on and watch for:

FIREBRICKS—At the back and sides of the stove, firebricks protect the body of the woodstove from intense heat. If a brick is broken, replace it; a damaged brick can cause the stove to crack or distort.

FIRE ROPE—Fitted around the door, this flameproof rope is designed to create a snug seal. Replace any missing or frayed rope and check that the door closes tightly. Trap a piece of paper in the door—it should resist being pulled out.

GLASS—A cracked glass screen needs replacing immediately, but it's an easy fix. Unscrew the tabs that keep it in place, measure the original glass, and order replacement stove glass online or from a local glazier.

RUST—Exterior rust can conceal hidden problems. Remove rust with a wire brush and refinish with stove paint. Keep the interior rust free by leaving the vent or door open during the summer months to encourage airflow.

CRACKS OR GAPS—Look for cracks on the stove body or between the side and top plates. Never use a woodstove that could leak fumes—it'll need professional attention from a qualified engineer.

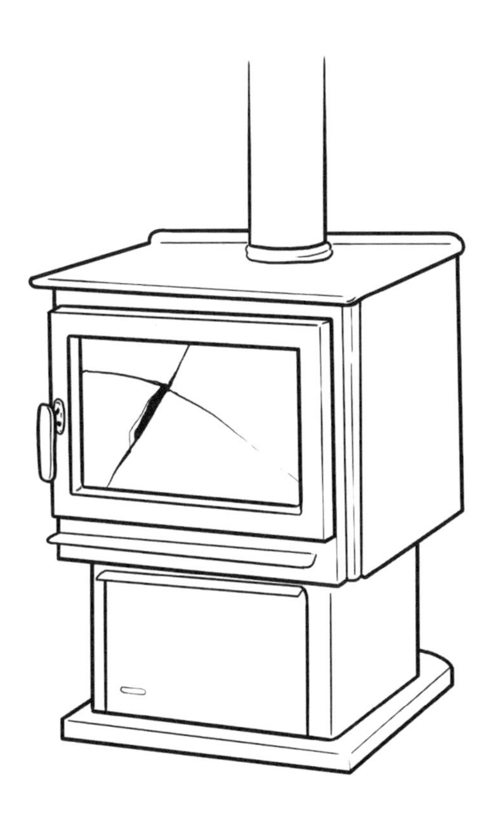

TIMBER TABLE

	HARDWOOD OR SOFTWOOD	FIREWOOD QUALITY	AROMATIC SMOKE
APPLE	Hardwood	Good	Yes
ASH	Hardwood	Excellent	Yes
BEECH	Hardwood	Excellent	
BIRCH	Hardwood	Very good	Yes
CEDAR	Softwood	Very good	Yes
CHERRY	Hardwood	Good	Yes
ELM	Softwood	Excellent	Yes
EUCALYPTUS	Hardwood	Good	Yes
HAWTHORN	Hardwood	Very good	

SEASONING TIME	GREEN BURNING	NOTES
1–2 years		Burns well with plenty of heat and no sparking. Sweetly fragranced smoke.
1 year	Yes	Burns well with plenty of heat and flames and no sparking. Splits easily with an axe.
1–2 years		Burns well with few sparks. Needs a long seasoning. Good for embers.
1 year	Yes	Burns well but fast. Best mixed with a slower fuel such as oak. Bark is great for tinder and kindling.
6–12 months	Yes	Burns well but fast. Deliciously fragranced smoke. Can green-burn small pieces.
1–2 years		Burns well with few sparks. Sweetly fragranced smoke.
2 years		Good, lasting heat and burns slowly. Not too many sparks. Needs a long seasoning.
1 year		Burns fast with a pleasantly fragrant smoke; not too many sparks.
1–2 years		Not readily available as a firewood but burns slow and hot with few sparks.

	HARDWOOD OR SOFTWOOD	FIREWOOD QUALITY	AROMATIC SMOKE
HAZEL	Hardwood	Very good	Yes
HOLLY	Hardwood	Good	
HORNBEAM	Hardwood	Excellent	
HORSE CHESTNUT	Hardwood	Poor	
MAPLE (INCLUDING SYCAMORE)	Hardwood	Good	Yes
OAK	Hardwood	Excellent	Yes
PINE	Softwood	Good	Yes
SPRUCE	Softwood	Good	Yes
SWEET CHESTNUT	Hardwood	Good	
WALNUT	Hardwood	Good	Yes

SEASONING TIME	GREEN BURNING	NOTES
1 year		Not readily available as a firewood but burns fast without many sparks.
1 year	Yes	A fast-burning, moderate-heat firewood that can be burned green if necessary.
2 years		Burns well. Not many sparks. Excellent embers.
1–2 years		Burns moderately to poorly. Difficult to split. Unpleasant-smelling smoke.
6–12 months	Yes	Burns quite hot with plenty of flames. Not prone to sparks.
2 years		One of the best firewoods. Gives off a good, lasting heat and burns slow and hot. Produces lots of ash.
1 year		Sooty and prone to sparks but good for kindling.
1 year		Low quality but fine for kindling.
1–2 years		Prone to excessive sparks. Not for use in a fireplace but burns well.
1 year		Burns well but quite quickly. Lovely-smelling smoke.

RESOURCES

For more information on North American fire regulation, fire safety, and wood burning stoves consult the following sources:

GENERAL FIRE SAFETY INFORMATION FOR THE UNITED STATES

National Fire Protection Association fire safety and fire prevention advice: *nfpa.org*

U.S. Fire Administration: *usfa.fema.gov/prevention*

American Red Cross home fire safety tips: *redcross.org/get-help/how-to-prepare-for-emergencies/types-of-emergencies/fire*

Biomass Energy Resource Center: *biomasscenter.org*

BurnWise: *epa.gov/burnwise*

Chimney Safety Institute of America: *csia.org*

Department of Energy: *energy.gov*

National Chimney Sweep Guild: *ncsg.org*

National Fireplace Institute: *nficertified.org*

U.S. Forest Service: *fs.fed.us*

WOODSTOVE MANUFACTURERS IN THE UNITED STATES

Appalachian Stove: *appalachianstove.com*

Blaze King Industries: *blazeking.com*

Buck Stove: *buckstove.com*

Hearth and Home Technologies: *hearthnhome.com*

Hearthstone: *hearthstonestoves.com*

Jøtul North America: *jotul.com/us/home*

Pacific Energy: *pacificenergy.net*

United States Stove Company: *usstove.com*

Vermont Castings: *vermontcastings.com*

Woodstock Soapstone Company: *woodstove.com*

GENERAL FIRE SAFETY INFORMATION FOR CANADA

Biomass Innovation Centre: *biomassinnovation.ca*

Canada Fire Safety Association: *canadianfiresafety.com*

Canadian Council of Ministries of the Environment: *ccme.ca/en/*

Chimney Safety Institute of America: *csia.org*

Fire Marshal's Public Fire Safety council: *firesafetycouncil.com/about-us*

Wood Energy Technical Training: *wettinc.ca*

WOODSTOVE MANUFACTURERS IN CANADA

Drolet: *drolet.ca/en/*

Lopi: *lopi.ca*

Osburn: *osburn-mfg.com/en/*

Napoleon: *napoleonfireplaces.com*

Northwest Stoves: *northweststoves.ca*

Regency Fireplace Products: *regency-fire.com*

Sherwood Industries: *sherwoodindustries.ca*

Timberwolf: *timberwolffireplaces.com*

Wilk Stove: *wilkstove.com*

INDEX

AUTHOR

S. Coulthard, discouraged at a young age from entering a career in professional pyromania, is an author of design and outdoor living books, architect and builder of garden structures, and a farmer in the north of England.